Life in the World Hereafter

Life in the World Hereafter

The Journey Continues

Gregge Tiffen

P-Systems
La Jolla, California

Publisher's Note: We would like to thank each of you who have helped make it possible to publish the autographed First Edition of *LIFE IN THE WORLD HEREAFTER: The Journey Continues* through your advance orders.

P-Systems
P. O. Box 12754
La Jolla, California 92039-2754

Fifth Printing
ISBN: 978-0-9754494-5-5

www.g-systems.com

To Bonnie

Whose support and conviction
found a pathway through every obstacle
which allowed this work to find its rightful conclusion.

Dallas, Texas
2006

People pay for what they do, and still more for what they have allowed themselves to become, and they pay for it very simply, by the lives they lead.

— James Baldwin

Contents

Acknowledgments

I thank those wonderful souls on the other side who so graciously embraced this effort with their love, affection, and wisdom.

I thank Patricia Florin for her patience and editorial guidance which gave this book coherence and meaning to all of us in need of the message.

I thank PJC and MCC for their generosity, support, and encouragement throughout the development of the project.

I thank Patrece and Julie for willingly tackling the myriad needs and demands, often at the expense of their valuable time, energy, and assets regardless of the thousand-plus miles that separated us.

And most of all to my mother who, although gone from this world, never left my side when her grace and guidance was needed.

Introduction

To die will be an awfully big adventure.

—Sir J.M. Barrie
Peter Pan

What if I told you that your intelligence, talent, and skill qualified you to attend a most prestigious university? What if I told you that you could attend on a full scholarship, study only what you wished, and had at your disposal the best, brightest, and most willing experts? What if I told you that at the end of the experience you would walk out of that school feeling a sense of not only accomplishment but awe at the knowledge you will have acquired?

It's all true. Every one of us is a willing participant in one of the grandest opportunities in the Universe—an experience offered only by this unique, challenging, and prestigious Earth School.

There is much more to us than most of us realize, although that may be hard to believe when we're suffering pain or performing a thankless task. Understandably, we get so caught up in the rudiments of living in a physical world where we have to find, prepare, and eat food, maintain a body, take care of others, and pay bills, that it is easy to let ourselves fall prey to fears and anxieties as we come up against obstacles. The obstacle that brings out our most visceral fears is the mystery of what happens after we die.

As spiritual beings searching for wisdom, we thrive on mystery. Our libraries, movies, laboratories, and lives are filled with them. Mysteries enliven and engage us as we

question, search, and piece together their meaning. Then, as
we bask in newly found clarity, more questions emerge, more
mysteries await. Even the mystery of death can become so
enticing that we flirt with death just to have a peek. But to the
physical body we have settled into for this learning
experience, death is seen as a bully, a thief, life's greatest
enemy.

Because we haven't been able to stop death, we try not to
think about it. After all, what else can we do? Most of us
manage to slip ourselves into a state of complacency where
we can usually be unmindful that our lifetime here will come
to an end. In the words of Morrie Schwartz in *Tuesdays with
Morrie*, "Everyone knows they're going to die, but nobody
believes it."[1] Denial may offer us a pleasant respite from fear
for a time, but reality will have its way.

As human-spiritual beings, we have lost our connection
to that which is beyond this physical life and have fallen into
fear about life in the hereafter. Rather than living to satisfy
our deeper desires and participate in joyful and intelligent
learning, for too many of us this fear of death is so large and
overwhelming that it has become the motivator behind our
life choices.

We *can* know what happens after we die. That we can't is
the first of many myths I wish to debunk. The world on the
other side has unveiled itself to me many times, and I'm not
alone. Perhaps you have seen the other side but have been
too alarmed or unable to recognize what you were
experiencing. Communicating with the discarnate is
something we are all capable of if we put in the study and
work. There are those of us who have done the work and are
able to access life in the hereafter fairly easily. We are talking,

---

[1] Mitch Albom, *Tuesdays with Morrie* (New York: Doubleday, 1997),
p. 81. Schwartz also said, "Learn how to die, and you learn how to
live" (p. 83).

and hope you are listening, because this tremendous fear of death—and if we look deeply enough, that is where most of our fears are rooted—hinders our development as human-spiritual beings, individually and collectively, by misdirecting life force we could be using for more creative endeavors. If we understood death and the reason for it, if we knew what to expect in the hereafter, we could appreciate the life we have and make it a deep and satisfying adventure.

My own introduction to life in the hereafter came, as it has for many, with a near-death experience. When I was nineteen years old, I had typhus and lay in a coma for twenty-three days. At some point during that time, my consciousness left my body and floated near the ceiling. I was able to look down at my body, hooked up to the usual things they used in intensive care at the time, and watch as the nurses and doctors came and went. I felt no sense of urgency to get back, no fear or excitement, not even an urge to evaluate for myself what was going on. I just accepted it as an experience. I was convinced that I was dead, and that was okay with me. Then I turned and looked up and saw an exquisite light, and I was filled with music far more glorious than anything I'd ever heard. I warmed myself in its depth and beauty and began to move into the welcoming brilliance of the light when a voice said, "You can't stay." I continued moving forward into the light, and the voice again said, rather sternly this time, "You can't stay."

My next recollection was being back in my body and terribly disappointed. Although my life hadn't been bad, it wasn't so terrific that I was grateful to have it back. I did not want to exchange the free-floating lightness and the beauty of the light and sound for the heaviness and weakness of my ailing body. I'd lost thirty-eight pounds in just over three weeks. There was a lot of rebuilding to do, and it took months of rehabilitation. I often thought about the place I almost went, especially on rough and rotten days.

Based on the warmth and welcome of my near-death experience, I was not only convinced that there was life after death, but I believed it to be a pretty good place. Even now when I struggle with the body, with its limitations and heaviness, I can get impatient to get out of this world and into the next. Then I remember what else the experience showed me. It helped me to see that there are things for me to do here, gifts to receive. It's like going to a party, having one drink, and then leaving. Why would you do that? You wouldn't. You'd stick around and receive the gifts of enjoyment. I think that if everyone over the age of fifty could have the experience of going to that part of the hereafter and coming back, this would be a very different world. We would realize that there is no longer anything to fear. We would be more confident in exercising our responsibility and power over ourselves and more compassionate and generous in how we view life.

ONE

Stepping Over the Threshold

...and therefore, never send to know for whom the bell tolls; it tolls for thee.

—John Donne
Devotions

One evening after my tour of duty in Korea and while I was still in the service, my wife and I went to a friend's house. She and some of the other wives were meeting with a medium, and she begged me to go. When we got there, my friend Smitty and I hung out in the kitchen drinking beer while the four women sat around a table in the other room to conduct a séance. They cajoled us to come and join them. Finally, and reluctantly, I put down my beer and wandered in.

The medium was a heavyset woman named Mary who'd been doing this for a long time. Only four could fit at the square table, similar to a card table only sturdier, so one of the women got up and gave me her seat. The others at the table were Mary, my wife, and Smitty's wife. Mary told us all to put our hands on the table but not to let them touch anyone else's. As soon as I put my hands on the table, it began to rock and bounce a couple of inches off the floor. Everyone was excited and a bit scared. I thought it was great.

Then a woman appeared on my right. I realized she was my mother. I had been the youngest of her three children, with six years' difference between the oldest and me. After I was born, she had never been well, and when I was two, she died. An aunt took care of me for the first couple of years after my mother died, until my father remarried a woman who I compared to the Frozen Witch of the North. Now I was feeling my mother enfold me in radiant, loving energy. I felt like a small child being taken up on his mother's lap and hugged.

The purpose of most séances is to ask questions, such as will I make money, when will I get out of the army, or does so-and-so love me. I had no urge to ask her questions, and it didn't appear that anyone else at the table could see her or feel the radiance. I didn't tell anyone at the time what I was seeing or feeling. It felt too personal.

She left, and more entities started to come through—all positive and one at a time—some of them relatives of those who were there. The table would move and rock, and somebody, usually Mary, would ask, "Who do we have?" If one of us recognized the discarnate, we would tell the others, "Oh, this is my Aunt Gloria." Another person came through for me that same night: Uncle John, my mother's brother. He had been a caretaker of the Wanamaker Estate in upstate New York. Occasionally, we used to visit him, his wife, and my cousin on weekends. Uncle John was the last person I would have thought of as a contact, so it was his appearance that convinced me something was really going on here and made it impossible for me to view the experience of seeing my mother as just a figment of my imagination.

The table kept tipping, and Mary kept asking questions. I was fascinated. How was this possible? What was making this happen? Here we were, all military, sitting in the living room on a military base talking to ghosts. The others were looking at me like I was Mr. Freaky and wondering what was going on. The whole thing lasted twenty minutes from the time my mother came through until we broke it off.[2]

---

[2] I do not recommend that anyone make a practice of participating in table-tipping sessions. The karmic ramifications for all concerned far exceed the benefit of information transmitted under such conditions.

At home, I told my wife about seeing my mother standing next to me and of her radiant embrace and then about receiving confirmation through Uncle John's appearance. It was such an immense and complete experience that I knew it hadn't been faked. This was one of those times that you know what you know, and I knew this was real. But how? I went to sleep that night feeling I'd entered a strange but welcome world. It was a comfortable feeling, like this was how things were supposed to be.

I felt strange the next day, but happy, and with a strong sense that I had crossed a threshold that was meant for me to cross. But I had questions, lots of them. I didn't like it that there didn't seem to be any answers or substance to this event. My educational background was in engineering, and I believed there were no phenomena, that everything had a fundamental explanation.

I went over to Mary's to see if she could answer my questions. I explained that I wanted to know how this could be. How could people who had been dead for years communicate with the living, and what had I done to create such activity at the séance? Happy to see me, she talked about discarnate entities who could come through, and she gave me general information that I could have read in any magazine. These were not the answers I was looking for, so she gave me the names of other people I could talk to about it. One of them was a medium in Chicago. He gave me more information about séances and table tipping and some reasonable explanations of energy and how it worked. He told me that discarnates come through the channel and that it is their energy connecting with the medium's energy that causes the table to tip. He also pointed out that answers given to the questions asked during séances are not necessarily valid. After all, if Uncle Harry drove a truck all his life, what would he know about the stock market?

Still shaken yet captivated with the wonderful but confusing nature of what had happened, I figured that I ought to be able to make this happen myself. A couple of days after the séance, I went up to my bedroom in the peace and quiet of the afternoon to see what would happen if I tried on my own. I lay down on the bed and focused. I already had the ability to focus intensely for long periods. When I coupled that with my new exposure to what was possible, I soon found that if I concentrated, it was easy for me to actually see the discarnate side. I did not wish, however, to contact my mother again, for two reasons: First, not only had that experience been complete in itself, but I felt it would have been a bit immoral to bring her back, because I understood that the sole purpose of her appearance was to open a door for me. She had indeed opened a door. This newfound ability was amazing, exciting, and had completely captured my attention. If I had wanted to see Uncle John again, I could just focus on him and either make contact mentally or see him. I was also contacting and conversing with many discarnate souls.

When I was upstairs in the bedroom, I received etheric visits, usually from a man, and was given instruction on psychic and mystical subjects, such as how to use my energy and what to do with it. It was explained to me that my life from then on was going to be different. Everything began to change, and I could feel the transformation mentally, physically, and of course, spiritually. I started a journal to record what I was doing. The very first line I wrote was, "I think I'm going crazy."

Finally understanding that I was clairvoyant, I felt I had no choice but to learn more about my ability. I was given information about the next step, and I would follow it. Many types of psychic abilities became available to me. Now that I knew I could do it, I was satisfied to do it just for my own purposes, for the thrill, the peace, and the answers it gave me.

I didn't hold séances or become a medium, since I lacked definition between the two. I hardly ever talked about it, except occasionally with my wife, and even then, not much.

Yet I still wanted to know how I was able to do this. I saw it as an engineering problem—how did energy transmit and transfer? It wasn't even a question of whether I was actually seeing the discarnate side—I knew I was—but how did it work within the context of what we knew about energy? Reading everything I could get my hands on and writing to people whom I thought could answer my questions, I came to the conclusion that if I was going to find my answers, it wouldn't be in the United States. I would have to go someplace where this kind of contact with the discarnate was very much an accepted and highly developed practice, not just an occasional odd incident. The East.

By this time, my wife and I had separated. I was still a captain in the army, but realized that I no longer belonged in that cut-and-dried world. A new and quite different life was being offered to me, one that was far more exciting. I felt as if I were peering into the core of a larger truth and being offered an opportunity to explore our biggest mystery—the very nature of beingness. I became consumed with following this new path and finding answers. Always methodical, I tried to plan what to do next, but only two steps were obvious to me: Resign from the military; and go someplace where they acknowledged and worked with the human energy system, studying how it functioned in this world and the next. I resigned from the army, and within a few months, I had arrived at an airport in India.

"Now what?" was not a question I asked, for I was learning that with each step I took, the next step would present itself to me. It was still quite a different format of operating than I was accustomed to, but it worked. At the airport I was met by a man who led me to his car, and we drove to a town near the border of Tibet. He dropped me off at a house where they gave me dinner and a place to sleep. The next day another man showed up and took me to the Tibetan border. No discussion took place, and no decision was made that this was where I would go. They just kept showing up, and I kept following. I never felt threatened, just destined. From the Tibetan border onward, it was horseback. We traveled a day and a night, never stopping for long. Not only did I feel as though I was in another country, but it felt as though I was in a different world.

I was taken to a monastery. This monastery did not focus on a religious practice. Its purpose was learning, and they were not monks but teachers. There was a mixture of races — some fair-skinned and blond, some dark-skinned and dark-haired. It was difficult to pinpoint ages. None of them looked older than sixty. Most of them wore robes and had beards. They were kindly yet serious. No fooling around.

They took me to what would be my room — a small, bare space with pinkish walls; a mattress filled with soft material on a raised platform; candles; and matches. They gave me a change of clothes, showed me where I could relieve myself, and left me there unattended, only bringing in food and taking away the empty dish from the day before.[3]

Days later a person of some standing showed up in the late afternoon and directed me to follow him out of the building and onto the grounds. He didn't explain anything, but I already understood that I was not being accepted on sight. They wanted to see if I had the psychological toughness and self-discipline they required before they offered me their teaching. It was also a test of my devotion and commitment to what I had set out to accomplish. That meant, in a most stringent way, being left alone in a cave and without contact for weeks on end, living in a strange

---

[3] It's important to clarify that no mind-altering substances were ever used in my training or in my work thereafter.

environment and, of course, without the things I was used to, like indoor plumbing or electric lights. They were making it as hard as possible, without being harmful or abusive, to see if I would quit. I had to prove myself, my willingness, and my ability. Without the discipline I'd learned in the army, I'm not sure I would have gotten through that time.

After that a handsome teacher in his early to mid-forties, as best I could guess, was assigned as my primary teacher. He determined my curriculum, and the other teachers operated within his plan. They began to teach me how energy works. Often they wouldn't even ask questions. I was expected to know the questions they wanted asked, as well as the answer. The point of teaching in this manner was to show me that I could do this myself and for them to evaluate how far I was progressing. The basis of their teaching was this: What is true of the part is true of the whole. They taught me the parts, explaining, demonstrating, and practicing with me, showing me that if I could understand how one molecule works, I could understand how all molecules work and how to use energy. "If it is true of the part, it is true of the whole" has remained the basis for everything I have ever learned since then.

Interestingly, I never met another student there. There may have been others; I just didn't meet any. I was not allowed outside the building during the day, only at night, on horseback, for exercise or instruction. The Chinese were getting closer, and although a person could pass within two hundred yards of this remote monastery and still not see it, perhaps the presence of an American, and a former soldier at that, would have brought problems to the monastery when the Chinese did finally arrive.

It was understood from the beginning that I would be returning to my country to use this teaching. Almost two years from the time I arrived in Tibet, I returned to the United States to work with people as I continued my studies.

Astral travel is the ability to separate one's consciousness from the physical body and travel to other locations. The body is slowed down to a minimal level of functioning to allow the energy body, or light body as it is called by some, to operate independently. The five physical senses are dulled, there is no muscle activity, nerve activity is low, and the heart rate drops. Although many travel astrally in their dream state, they usually don't remember it. The astral travel I do is carried out in a conscious way — begun awake, intentionally, with a destination in mind, and always in control.

When you are in this physically suspended state, loud or sharp noises nearby or other interruptions can be forceful enough to break the attachment to the physical body, so I always choose a time when there will be no interference — usually late afternoon. When release of the light body from the physical body occurs, the silver cord is visible. The silver cord is that energetic tether that connects your light body to your physical body.

Over the Earth are layers and layers of energy that must be passed through to accomplish the travel. Closest to Earth are the layers that hold negativity. These can cause the astral traveler the most trouble. This is the earthbound plane, the place where one finds those who have died but still cling to their heavy negativity — violence, depression, hunger for power, and always fear. (The earthbound plane is explained in more detail in later chapters.) Passing through here is like passing through hell. Conscious astral travel can be scary, which is probably why it isn't done much. Although I personally don't know of a case, I have heard that people have died doing it. I was taught about the dangers and shown how to sidestep them.

How often I met with my teacher depended upon my need for information. When there was something that I needed help with, I would choose a time when I knew there would be no interference — no telephone, no one knocking on the door — and lay on the bed and put myself into the state of physical non-feeling. Then I imaged the monastery in Tibet and my teacher and focused on them. At first it would take me almost a half-hour before I would find myself in front of him. But with practice, one develops skill, and it becomes a familiar process.

I also physically returned to Tibet two more times on extended stays for more extensive training to broaden the information and methodology. My complete training time encompassed six years. Although my learning has never stopped, it came to a point where I was kicked out of school, so to speak, and told to go and do my own thing. As is true for all of us, I was expected to keep learning through my experiences, and guidance and help have always been there when I've asked for them.

I had the ability to do almost anything that fell within the psychic realm, but I quickly realized that working that way was too scattered and unproductive. So I sat myself down and asked how I was going to use my abilities. I decided to do life readings. Just as you can see an electrical pulse pattern, I can see people's energy patterns, and I can read meaning from that pattern. Through astral travel, I am able to enter their energy space, overlay my own cells over theirs, and for a few moments gather information about them from the energetic plane. Then we talk about what I saw and what it means in terms of their present attitudes, behaviors, and the general direction of their life. I am able to give people enough vital information about themselves and their life task so that if they take it to heart and use it, they can further their self-knowledge. Although I have done other metaphysical work, including the astral rescue work I describe in chapter 7, life energy readings have been my primary focus.

By this time, my wife and I had divorced, and from the standpoint of what was considered normal, my life was pretty screwed up. Looking back, it's still amazing to me how

I managed to exist. I didn't have a so-called regular job but counseled people for a whopping five dollars an hour. I was driving from Carmel to Los Angeles on weekends to give lectures on metaphysical topics. If I had five people, that was a big night. Often I was faced with an empty room. But people gave me money and helped out, so I always seemed to have enough to get by. I lived in a house in Carmel but didn't have to pay rent, thanks to Dearie, a friend who owned a gift shop in Carmel and knew more about what was going on with me than anyone else. She also supplied a car when I didn't have one.

Different things began to happen to call attention to my work. There was a radio program in the 1970s hosted by Hilly Rose. Hilly had heard me as a guest on another late-night radio show and asked if I'd come on his program, which ran from midnight to five in the morning. He wanted me to talk about what I did and answer questions from listeners. I was on his show several times as well as other radio and television programs. I was also approached by the parapsychology department at UCLA. They wanted to do a serious investigation of my abilities, but they went about it like a witch hunt. After a couple of months, I stopped working with them. For a while, I became fairly well known in California. I was interviewed on several programs, even *Sheriff John*, an afternoon TV show for kids. I thought it interesting that a kids' show in the United States was covering the topic of past lives.

Perhaps the most memorable program I was on was *The Regis Philbin Show*, hosted in the Los Angeles area. I'd been on his show about four times when he asked if I would perform a table-tipping séance on TV. I agreed. We set it up in the studio, held the séance, and the table did its usual thing. During the program, someone said that it was fine and dandy as long as I was at the table, but maybe I had some trick that made the table move. So we took a couple of cameramen and studio people and put them at the table. I stood by to give basic instructions. Of course, the table started moving without me there, which freaked everyone out. A week or so later, the station got a letter from the FCC. It stated that the station could talk about a séance as a possibility and as research, but they could not put one on the air and present it as valid. That was the end of my experience with TV.

Turnout for my classes grew, so I expanded my teaching and lecturing schedule throughout California. I also started teaching in Dallas and Boston. It seemed like I was always on an airplane. My lectures covered a wide range of metaphysical topics such as meditation; understanding and expanding cellular energy; the structure of consciousness; the Law of Cause and Effect; a mystical view of discipline; the art of thinking; relationships; reducing stress; and more. It wasn't until the early 1990s that I cut back dramatically on my lecturing. I was tired. Now living in Dallas, I turned my focus back to doing private sessions as well as working with Bonnie Beck, my life mate of eighteen years, to get this work out into the world.

Before that first séance, I could never have conceived of a life where I would be tapping into the energetic realm for information and talking to people about their life lessons, previous lives, and life in the hereafter just as naturally as we might talk about our jobs or the weather. In the four decades since I have been back from Tibet, I have dealt with thousands of people, and I have a deep and vested interest in everyone I work with. The work carries commensurate karmic responsibility. I am responsible for giving people accurate information about their energy patterns, and if I tell them the wrong thing, I will have to pay for it karmically. All of us get back exactly what we put out. Karmic involvement cannot be denied. So while in everyday life I'm just as human and make just as many mistakes as others, I have found that I'm infallible when I do this work.

Eighty years of age now looms on my horizon, and I find myself getting disheartened when I see the foolishness of the human race; when I see the thoughtlessness and cruelties we perpetrate on one another; and when I see how we try to control and restrain others, spreading oppression like an out-of-control wildfire. I don't think that most people understand what life is about or that death is a natural transition into and an extension of this life. If they did, this world would be vastly different. As it is, too many people let fear and ignorance have their way with them, and the most fundamental fear revolves around the issue of death. We cannot truly appreciate the wonders and opportunities life offers us in every moment until we quit fretting about death and fearing it as a dark force that will end us. It is time to break through the mystery we have created around it.

In this lifetime, I have spent almost as much time in the discarnate as in the incarnate. I tell you with absolute certainty that we do not end with death, but we continue in a world that is much like this one, albeit with some profound differences. The incarnate and discarnate worlds make up the two sides of what I call the Earth School, and we have multiple lifetimes on both sides. In this book, I explain the two sides of the school and what to expect from the death experience itself and of life in the world hereafter. I also relate cautionary tales, drawn from documented astral rescue sessions. I suggest ways we can plan to die well, and I discuss my views on grief. I describe the realm that I call the nature pool. Finally, I talk about what I call "graduation" — that time when we have learned all we have come to learn in this school — and what lies beyond it.

I hope you find the information enlightening, helpful, and uplifting. If it is read with an open mind, it will, I hope, ease your fear of death and inspire you in the art of living.

Living well is, after all, the most important task that lies
before every one of us.

TWO

The Earth School

Is it possible that I am not alone in believing that in the dispute between Galileo and the Church, the Church was right and the centre of man's universe is the earth?

—Stephen Vizinczey
Hungarian novelist, critic

This sphere on which we live, breathe, dig, build, plant, and fish, where we engage one another in war and love, struggle and celebration, boredom and passion, is only part of the story of Earth and its people. The rest of the tale lies beyond what our five senses tell us. It is where we go when we die. Before explaining the other half of the Earth School, it would be helpful to put into perspective how we fit into the larger system.

As most of us go about our everyday lives, what we experience is really more "doing" than it is living. There's a big difference. In just doing, it is impossible for us to know that we are a part of Omnipotent Intelligence. Yet eventually each of us comes to a time when, as a result of events or experiences, we reach out to the Universe—whether we call it God or something else—as the source. When we do, we awaken that part of ourselves that recognizes the fundamentals of life, and we start to feel alive. We then manifest that feeling into action, and that action moves us to embrace the infinitude of the Universe by becoming an aware, living part of that reality.

By feeling our body through pleasure and pain, we learn that we *are*. That's why if we take powerful drugs to immobilize our senses, we cannot connect to the Universal action. Yet only our physical being is affected. We cannot immobilize our consciousness. Because what is true of the part is true of the whole and because our consciousness is part of the Universal whole, we have no power to stop it.

So we need to understand that the Universe is ever unfolding. It is infinite. It is in a constant state of discovery, it knows no limitations, it has no boundaries—and we are a part of that reality, unfolding on infinite levels, discovering on never-ending plateaus, forever moving upward and outward.

Physical life is only a small part of that process of discovery. Perhaps that is why we find ourselves on such a small planet. Apparently we don't need much room to discover the physical self. When we master that small exercise, we will leave Earth and go on to another school. The lessons never cease; they only become more fascinating and more exciting. Every answer produces another question. That is the Law of Infinity.

Each galaxy within the Universe is its own university with its own overall teaching pattern. Celestial bodies or "colleges" within the galaxies take the overall teaching pattern and break it down into separate studies, with each celestial body teaching an individual part of the pattern. Our own galaxy is uniquely set up by the Universe to teach adaptability.

Everything on Earth is in a state of change. Nothing remains constant. Pay attention for a moment, and see how everything within this moment is changing—you inhale, then exhale; sensations roam your body; sounds change course; and whatever you are looking at is changing before your eyes, molecule by molecule, microsecond by microsecond. Every thought, every conversation, every relationship is in a state of flux. The system that was good on Monday is being changed on Tuesday. Our dollars bills and buildings are deteriorating. Our bodies are changing and dying—the cells are breaking down, and some are being repaired and replaced, some are not. Change is our constant.

Our lesson is to learn to let go—to stay constantly changeable in our life. We do a lot of that without thinking about it. Eating and digestion change our food from one form into energy and waste products. When we go to sleep at night, many changes take place. Some we sense when get up in the morning, and some we do not. Changes are taking place in our bodies on a cellular level. Life is designed so that every conceivable incident and avenue of experience has a purpose—to teach us how to adapt. Once we comprehend that our lesson is adaptability, we are in concert with the teaching lesson of the school.

Adaptation is not to be confused with giving up. Adapting means finding out what the situation requires, then learning how to meet it. Remember when you were a child and had to learn the fundamentals of getting along on the planet? Take tying your shoes, for example. You probably fussed and fumed, maybe even shed a few tears over it, but eventually through application you learned how to do it. You did not give up—you adapted. The demand was this: Many shoes are made with shoelaces whether you like it or not, so you had better learn to tie them. Once you learned to tie your shoes, it was no longer an issue. It had become knowledge, and you no longer had to think about it.

You started to learn, probably by the time that you were five, that there were people out there—certain big people—who carried big sticks and who would sometimes use them on you. You learned that some people loved you, and some ignored you. You started seeing that the complexity of dealing with other people was something you either had to adapt to or try to avoid. When someone says, "I don't like confrontations, so I avoid them," that is not adapting. It is giving up through avoidance. Adaptation doesn't mean staying with a job you don't like. Adaptation doesn't mean living in a geographical area that doesn't please you. Again, that is giving up. Adaptation is taking control and learning how to assess and deal with each situation in such a way that you can move on. That experience then becomes knowledge, and you've progressed.

If you think you can't do this, you're wrong. Not only can you, but eventually you *must*. It makes no difference whether you do it in this particular sojourn or 100 million years from now in another, you have agreed to this task. You wouldn't be here if you hadn't, and you wouldn't be here if you weren't capable of succeeding. So sooner or later, you must learn, and all that you experience on this planet will be transformed into knowledge.

We progress by experiencing what is happening with our full awareness. We should never go through any condition or event without perceiving the full essence of that experience through our own senses. When was the last time you really *tasted* a French fry? When was the last time you watched a television commercial and paid attention to the layers of voices, sounds, and music and how they framed the characters, relationships, and product? (You can bet the makers of it did.) When was the last time you really looked at the area within five feet of your front door? Or looked deep into your loved one's eyes? What is going on in your body right now?

Once we register an experience, we have a reaction: I have had this experience, and it has brought me to this point. That is knowledge. Every one of us is unique, and when we're paying attention, we bring our unique knowledge to the Universe. We know we're gaining knowledge when we have moments of discovery, those aha's! Even if a million others have already discovered what we're seeing, hearing, tasting, touching, or smelling, our own experience of it is always unique and always valuable.

Then, when we begin to know something so well—knowing it without knowing how we know—we have gained wisdom.

Experience = awareness = knowledge = wisdom™ is the sequence that brings us into living fully. The problem is that the process can appear to be a struggle. Every day, between the time you wake up and the time you go to bed, you will be up against tens of thousands to even hundreds of thousands of changes, many of which you will have to be cognizant of and most of which you will have to adapt to. Too big a job? Again, you wouldn't be here if you weren't up to the challenge. There are things you can do to get yourself in shape for the challenge. This school doesn't get easier just because you are less healthy physically, mentally, or spiritually.

Physically, it is our body that is our first line of contact with life experience, and it likes to dictate how life should be since, after all, it is the vehicle of the planet. The body is concerned with only one thing—survival. It sees change as dying and death, and it does not want to pass through changes, because it realizes that it must eventually reach the end of its function and stop. Take control of your body, and exercise your fundamental responsibility to operate this earth vehicle of yours at its most optimal to keep your senses sharp and your experiences vital. Eat properly, exercise, and treat your body with respect.

To foster both mental and spiritual health, maintain your individuality. Like the body, societies are concerned with only one thing—survival. To survive, they need members. Societies can serve important functions, but it is too easy to give ourselves over to them, either because we believe that doing so serves a higher purpose or because we are too lazy or frightened to claim and live our individuality. When we let society or culture determine what we should believe and how we live, we have abdicated our responsibility for ourselves.

We have given ourselves over to living a system, not to our individuality, and we do not learn. Unless we change that and live for ourselves, we will have to come back again to complete the assignment. Your only focus should be on your own quality, which is inevitably reflected in the world. If we all worked to improve our own quality, we would indeed improve society.

To foster your spiritual health, manifest what you believe to be your fundamental truth. This should be the motivator of everything you do. Even your mistakes have their initial source in your fundamental truth. The process of learning and growing through life is the highest value of truth.

The Earth School is a tough one, post-graduate level, and there is a condition here that can make things more difficult: This is a dual-sided school. The incarnate side of this school teaches one issue of adaptation. Then we die. When we die, the physical body ends, but consciousness goes on. However, it does not go off to dance upon the clouds but enters an astral state that is an integral part of this school. Many think that when they die they will be finished, and it will be playtime. No, we're still in school.

The other side of the school has no physical form, but it still has visual form. It is there where you learn another set of conditions assigned to this school of adaptability. The physical and non-physical sides mirror each other. On the incarnate side, we have schools, hospitals, and governments. On the discarnate side, there are schools, hospitals, and governments. The difference is that on the incarnate side we operate at a considerably lower level of capacity and function than on the discarnate side. Through reincarnation, we move back and forth between the two parts of the school.

When you graduate from here, you're going to have one hell of a diploma in your hand. Tough school, but every living being on this planet now, in the past, and in the future is qualified to be here. The learning is intricate, but we weren't sent to learn it in just one lifetime. If we approach it a day at a time, a step at a time, it's manageable. We look at the lesson directly in front of us at any given moment, and that's all we have to be concerned with. How fast or slow we move is determined by the Universe. As we produce the result of any part of the lesson, the Universe will move us at an economical rate to where we're supposed to be next.

Rewards? You better believe it! In this system, every act you commit ends up as knowledge. That is life! Life is the reward. And if you groaned when you read that, it means you have not yet discovered the richness, depth, and ecstasy of life here. Next, let's look at the transition that occurs at death.

THREE

Death Transition

Life is pleasant. Death is peaceful. It's the transition that's troublesome.

— Isaac Asimov

The most dramatic and difficult adaptation we confront in the Earth School of adaptability is that of death. Our attitudes and fears about death determine the very quality and depth with which we engage in life. Death is seen as the enemy. We portray it as a skeletal specter in a black cloak, scythe ready to sever us from our life and everyone and everything we hold dear. If death comes for us — and we often delude ourselves by thinking of it as *if*, not *when* — we do not know what, if anything, will happen next.

Fear of death is the legacy of generation upon generation of attempts to explain what we have forgotten about the other side of the Earth School. Religions trade on death. For thousands of years, we have based societies on a number of religious principles that have been predicated upon death and the fear of it. We are told that if we follow the religion's dogma, we will be rewarded when we die. If we do believe in a religion, that belief then puts us up against all the other concepts, philosophies, and religions that say something different. Within every square inch of what we call civilized humanity, a model of living has been formed based on the fear of dying. Few models have been based on the joy of living and the joy of dying. This terrible perpetuation of the mystery underwrites our folly, our weakness, and our fears. By not understanding what happens when we die, we waste a lot of time reacting to our fear rather than carrying on our purpose for living. Understanding the transition of death and what to expect on the other side will free us to embrace life.

When and How Will I Die?

Our moment of death is determined by our life learning lesson. At the moment of our birth, the life learning lesson we agreed to take on and the requirements for its completion were programmed into each and every one of our physical body cells. Death comes to us only when one of these three conditions takes place:

1) We have completed everything we came to do, as determined by the learning lesson we have taken on.

2) We simply cannot complete what we came to do as a result of circumstances or the way we have handled our life. Consciousness then decides to remove itself so it has an opportunity to come back and try all over again.

3) We believe we can supercede the laws of the Universe and decide to take our own life.

There are no other reasons we die. None. Now, there are differences in the way death is brought about. It may be sudden or lingering or experienced from a state of conscious awareness and timing. (Conscious death is discussed in chapter 8.)

In a lingering death—a person who suffers for years with cancer, for example—the individual may be cutting a partnership with pain. Although it is possible that the pain can be used to serve the life learning lesson in some way, elongated pain is a negative learning tool and has a severe effect on the consciousness. It is also likely that a person will die with the belief that because his or her life culminated in pain, all life is therefore painful. This belief must then be dealt with when the individual begins life on the other side of the Earth School. In a fundamentally harmonious Universe, lingering pain is not an efficient means to any end.

The person who experiences sudden death is usually confused because he or she has not had a chance to prepare for the transition. The person hit by a bus perceived his life as active and moving, and in a flash, it was gone. This would be the same condition, more or less, for those killed on a battlefield. These individuals make the transition either realizing that something has occurred and they are open to what might be on the other side (that is, someone to help them move on) or hanging around in the in-between, earthbound state knowing that things aren't right but with no idea of what to do about it or where to go.

The people killed in a plane crash were all on that plane for the same reason—it was time to go. Someone killed in battle was killed because it was time to go, and that happened to be the means. The terrible part is that we have developed horribly destructive means for making the transition. The only thing that's true in every death is that the body has to stop breathing. The elements and methodologies that lead up to that can be quite different.

The ideal way to die is to stay on task with the life learning lesson, and when we realize that we have run out the string—either we have completed the learning we came to do or we cannot complete it because of circumstances or how we have handled our life—we simply lie down, have a big yawn, and leave the body. Our consciousness makes the transition to the other side while our body stays here to be buried, cremated, or sent to a scientific institution for study. That way is so simple that it takes a lot of skill. So we find ourselves couching death in disastrous terms, dying from disease or violence and almost always against our will, as if it leaves behind a residue of sympathy and courage that makes us more memorable to those we leave behind. Those who die with true courage know they are not really facing death but life, the life on the other side of the Earth School. It is welcomed, not so much because it is better than what we have here, but because it is a natural continuation of what we have here.

The Life Timeline

Consciousness enters the body with the first breath of life and leaves the body with the final breath. In between is our life timeline. A life timeline is not measured in years. It is measured in the experience we have agreed to have. We do not have a set time—for example, seventy-seven years, three months and two days—in which to complete the experience. If you were to plot your own lifeline, putting "B" to represent the year you were born and stringing a line to "D" for the time of death, that same line could represent ten years or eighty-nine years. We are concerned with producing a pattern of experiences rather than an amount of time. The measurement of years is man-made and means nothing when it comes to determining our point of death. "D" is tied to the point at which the lesson either has been learned to the degree that it is complete or has not been learned and could not be learned even if circumstances were altered.

When we arrive at "B," the point of birth, our consciousness already knows the point of our death, that is, the point at which our learning experience will have reached its apex. As long as circumstances are such that we can still make progress, we will not die at any point short of that apex. This is why we can go through such terrible misery, even to the point of pleading with God to let us die, but keep on living. The answer to our pleading is that we are not yet at the apex, and we cannot leave this life because we haven't fulfilled the pattern of experiences in the life learning lesson. The child, the young person, or the middle-aged individual killed by some dastardly accident or enemy bullet was not cut down in the prime of life but had reached his learning apex or was as far as he was going to go as a result of circumstances.

What about the person who we claim has cheated death — the person who is seen fighting for life even up to what looks like the final moment before death — and lives? When we see someone who survives at the point of death as a result of struggle, who has fulfilled what we see as the law of survival, he is not doing what we might think. He is not cheating death in order to stay alive. He is grasping for answers, answers that have eluded him until that moment. He does not want to step across the threshold to the other side of life not knowing. The fight for survival is not a fight for life. It is a fight for an answer.

The answer we seek has to do with the agreement we made with the Universe, for we did not *decide* to come into this life to learn a lesson; we *agreed* to come in. Our agreement was based on information and facts presented to us by more advanced individuals who have the responsibility of explaining our life learning lesson, and we concurred. That agreement did not include our being able to determine how it should be; we just concurred with the information presented to us and agreed to take on the lesson.

Once here, some try to back out of the agreement by taking their own life. Suicide preempts the natural timing of the life, and taking action to terminate life is the ultimate transgression against this infinite Universe. None of us is in a position to take a life. Only Omnipotent Intelligence, God, can decide that. An individual who suicides is in a self-inflicted state of blindness, refusing to see the options available to heal, and in taking his own life, he is trying to usurp the position of higher intelligence.

You might say, "Well, it's my life and I can do what I want with it, and right now I'm going to end it." But *you* wouldn't end. You can't. None of us has the power to stop the action of life in this infinite Universe. You just make a transition, minus the physical being, and your consciousness is still very much alive, very much aware, and fully capable of evaluating what went on. All you would have done is disturbed the outworking of the law by moving to the other side prematurely. You then have to come back to this side of the school to finish the life learning lesson you initially agreed to.

It is also possible to rush ourselves into circumstances in which there is no way we can learn our lesson in this life. We then have to leave, go to the other side, and prepare to do it all over again. Whenever we find ourselves ignoring the moment, losing track of ourselves and what we're here to do by clinging to distractions or ignorance, we are not learning. We are perpetuating misery and embracing death more quickly. By applying free will, many can, and often do, put themselves into situations that make the progress of their life learning lesson impossible to carry out. Abusing drugs or alcohol, breaking the law and being incarcerated, or inflicting harm on ourselves are examples of circumstances with no positive outcome. Who decides that? Fundamentally, we do, and in seeing how we have obstructed ourselves, we begin to make decisions that will lead to our "premature" death. We know when we have damaged ourselves beyond repair, and we begin to give up. That can bring about some terminal illness or put our body in harm's way. The "how" doesn't matter.

What directs us is the awareness that we have run out of options to continue the life experience in a spiritually acceptable format. No outside critic or guide is telling us that all is lost so give it up. It is an act of awareness, carried out by our soul, our consciousness, our spirit, that makes us see the vision of who we are, what we have become, and what we must do to change it and get back on track. This judgment takes place within us usually over a period of time. Although it can be a lightning-strike type of event that shocks us into awareness, most of the time this kind of shock changes our life and shows us how to get back on the path. Sometimes it doesn't move us at all because we believe we are too far gone for salvation. As always, we will make that decision and exercise our free will in manifesting whatever action we see as the next logical move.

We have free will, but we do not have the right to intercede with the will of the Higher Power. To do so is to break the Law. Because we did not create life, we have no right to take it away. Wars and accidents are perpetrated by humans and are the use of free will in its most negative form. If every accident that resulted in the loss of life were investigated in minute detail, we would find a point at which the individual responsible for the killing made a decision that was directly responsible for the incident. The person killed was there at that moment by choice. The obvious conclusion, then, is that there is no such thing as an accident. All parties are responsible for being where they are, with the means to kill and the free will to use those means against another human who has decided to be at that place at that time.

In everyday life there are inherent risks. Every time we cross the street, get on an airplane, eat, or carry out our daily chores, there is risk. At the level of physical consciousness, every one of us knows it. Sometimes one of those risks becomes the means by which we reach physical closure to our life learning lesson and current experience here on Earth. Other times it will provide an experience to give us an opportunity to learn more about ourselves and our life lesson. Let's look at the case of someone killed by a drunk driver. Did the victim plan his death to be that way? Perhaps not consciously, but before leaving home he knew, on some level, that his life was in threat. This would have been manifested at a deeper level through depression, anger, despondency, or exhaustion to a point that he was no longer able to motivate himself. In such a state, we can create within ourselves a condition where we are a potential victim. Had the individual known a drunk driver would be on that road at that time, he probably would have made a choice to be somewhere else. The results would have been the same — he would have died, although in some other way, because he put himself in a condition to end his current physical experience here on Earth. "Accidental" death can also occur when someone carries heavy guilt that has to be remedied in order to arrive on the positive side of the hereafter. He puts himself in a position of inflicting a traumatic life experience in the belief that doing so will balance the books in his favor when he arrives on the discarnate side of the school.

Because our society has no other means of explaining how these incidents can take place, we choose to call them accidents. Yet because free will never disengages itself from our consciousness, the parties involved were where they were by choice, not by chance. Does that make us co-conspirators in our death? Yes. While there can be dozens of reasons why we were at that place at that time, in that list of reasons we could find the one that was bound to make us a victim. As one poet said, "We are the captain of our ship, the master of our soul." It is not necessary for us to rush toward a point of death in a negative way. We can approach our apex of learning and then invite a soft, warm, easy, comfortable, and joyful transition.

What Happens When We Die?

We like to think that our moment of death will be a peaceful, harmonious return to our spiritual home, as it were, a place where the pain, effort, and intensity we know in this life are gone. That is possible. What is important to remember is that the quality of our death is directly determined by the quality of our incarnate life. That quality will be reflected into our death transition. Let's look at what happens at the moment of our transition from this life to the other side of the Earth School.

Mirror: Reflective Side–Opaque Side

The Universe put an interesting hand into making up this world of ours. If I drew a picture of the edge of a cell and enlarged it, we would see that the cell is actually multi-layered. This is both a physical cell and a cell as part of the energy of consciousness. Although consciousness does not actually have cells, it does have atomic structure.

Here is where the Universe has done an interesting thing. In order for all cells to function, they must function like mirrors. Picture a small round mirror. One side is reflective, and the opposite side is opaque. The reflective side shows us our current life experience. Our cells reflect everything we do, producing actions that we call experience. The only way our cells can have this reflective side is if their opposite side is opaque. Like every mirror, the cells must have silvering on the back to allow the front to be reflective. The opaque side of the cell will be shown to us after we die. That means that while we are on this side of the Earth School, the incarnate world is the reflected side. The discarnate side, the other side of our knowledge, is opaque. That is why we do not know on this side of the mirror, or school, about the other side. It is literally obscured.

To really know about the other side while we are incarnate, we must go to a supralevel. At a supralevel, the cell becomes like a sphere on which we cannot find either an opaque or a reflective side. In its full position, the cell is in an entwined condition, the opaque and reflecting aspects twisted together in such a way that you cannot tell what is opaque and what is reflective. It is all dark and all reflective at the same time. It is dark and light. That is when we can understand who we are, what we are, and where we are in terms of life/death. When that occurs, we can say we've got this whole question solved: There is no life, there is no death, but there is all life, there is all death, and we understand them as a unity. At that point, we give up chasing life or death. We give up fearing either of them, and we embrace our experience. This is transcendental awareness. Although rare, we are all capable of experiencing this state.

As you and I operate day to day, we operate within this cell structure that is reflective, and we cannot see the other side. It is helpful to remind ourselves that we are not dealing with life and death but with our self and the creative force.

Physical Signs of Transition

In the system of life and death reflection, some intriguing things take place. It is the life side of the cell, the reflection, that lets us know when we have arrived at the proper apex. It is the one that says either we are not going to accomplish the life learning lesson or we have completed it in the way we agreed, and it is time to make the transition to our next experience. Let's assume for this discussion that we are at the point when, somewhere in the next few days or weeks, we are going to cash in our chips, call it quits, and make our transition to another phase. At that point, two important events happen within the body.

First, all of our cells recognize the apex and communicate that to every bit of our being through all of our physical senses. Those readying to go to the other side of the school begin to dissociate themselves from the physical world. They become absent-minded. Things that were once important to them are no longer a priority. Relationships with people do not have the same meaning. Depending on the individual, he or she begins to forgive old hurts and wounds. There are some marked physical dysfunctions. Individuals who seemed to deal well physically now begin to function poorly: Their hearing goes, their sight goes, and above all, their coordination—both eye-hand and walking—starts to fall apart. They sleep less. When they're awake, they don't seem to be as bright as they used to be. They seem removed and preoccupied. Holidays become either very important or not important at all. In many cases, they become important because there is a tendency to set the transition time somewhere near an important date—a holiday, a birthday or an event such as a graduation or a wedding of someone close to them—a marker, as if to say they would like to stay around just until then.

We have a tendency to be ruled by the calendar, and in the eyes of the Universe, a few weeks or months more in the life pattern is not a problem. Although when it's time, it's time, regardless of what the calendar says. While you may have a few days, hours, or weeks to play with, there is a cut-off time that you cannot hold off. When you reach that cut-off time, no matter what, that's it.

There are those who are, in a sense, able to extend their experience here. The first way is by how time is experienced. A minute is a minute, sixty precise ticks on the clock. We cannot change that. Also built within each of us is our own time clock, and what those sixty seconds feel like to each of us depends on how we choose to experience that time. So we do have the means of making that sixty seconds seem different than what we imagine it to be by the clock. Although a tick of the clock is one second, you can extend that tick in terms of experience.

The other way people extend their physical time here is to go into a coma. We cannot control the moment of death, that is, the moment that consciousness leaves the body. Even though the body is in a coma, the consciousness is actually on the other side. We often say that someone in a coma for a long period of time is trying to hold on. No one can hold on to incarnate life once that cut-off time has been reached, but we can keep from moving on when we're on the other side of the Earth School. Such an individual would most likely be stuck in the earthbound or negative planes of the discarnate, which will be discussed later.

The second thing that occurs when preparing for the transition is that the body's cells begin to do an interesting flop. They start this pancake turn, a motion in which the reflective side now moves and exposes the opaque side. The opaque side becomes the reflective side. Coordination further deteriorates as the cells purposely lose stability. They are preparing consciousness to accept the transition, to be able to see the opaque-death side as the cells begin to face the discarnate. We can see this when someone goes into a comatose or semi-comatose state for a period of time before they die. If they come out of the comatose state at all, they talk about people they knew who had died as if those people were in the room. They talk about it as if it were real because it is real to them. They have had a chance to view the other side. At this particular point, the consciousness in the cells cannot distinguish between life incarnate and death discarnate. They are experienced as one and the same, a state completely different from either the incarnate or discarnate side alone. This is an in-between state that exists while preparing to make the transition.

This occurs for everyone, whether it is someone in the armed services heading out on military operations in which he is going to die or someone lying seriously ill in a hospital bed. Although the soldier is under a different, stressed condition, the disorientation and pre-death reaction are not at all dissimilar. The body is fighting desperately to go through this phase, to align itself and consciousness properly for the death transition. This alignment can take place in just fractions of a second or hours. This is why some people linger, regardless of their physical state. They can be lying there maimed and with body parts missing, and every cell in the body is fighting, not to live, but to prepare for transition by flipping and readying the individual to see both sides.

I've been asked if it still happens in someone who knows when they will die, someone being executed, for example. Yes, it does. We are all dominated by the status of the cells, and the process must still take place, regardless of whether the individual began the process days, hours, minutes, or even seconds before the execution. This is why someone can walk to his own execution with a great sense of calm and finality. He is calm because the cells have flipped, showing him the other side of life, and he has completely dissociated from his current experience.

The flipping of the cells also explains that flash of life before our eyes when we die; only, it's not our life we're seeing but *life* itself. As the cells are flipping, your experience of life here and life there is occurring at the same time, and what you have in that moment is an overwhelming sense of your entire life. This moment is the culmination of your understanding of your complete life experience.

The Three-Sided Mirror

There is an ideal state as we work toward the apex. As we move toward the apex, we can know exactly when we are in it. We can train ourselves to turn the mirror in a side direction instead of flipping over and up. When this movement occurs, some interesting things happen. Where it used to be a two-sided mirror (in which we had a reflective side and an opaque side), when a cell begins to turn in the other direction, the mirror takes on a third side. We then have a reflective side, an opaque side, and a neutral side. The neutral side incorporates knowledge of both the reflective and opaque sides. The person who does this is truly living a full life, with full awareness—not living life *then* death, not living life *or* death, but living life *and* death both. Such an individual would be a wise person, not for what he knows, but for how he lives. This person has all the qualities of life and death. This is, again, transcendental awareness.

Preparing to Die

As we prepare to be born, we work together with our mother on this side of the school. She is pregnant for nine months, and we, as a spiritual being, a consciousness, run parallel to the fetus so that at the proper time for birth our consciousness is joined with the body. In the last three months of this pregnancy and especially the last few weeks, our awareness of that parallel is strong. By the time of our birth, we are fairly knowledgeable about what is happening to the flow of activity and energy in the life/death system.

Of course, our mother is not part of our death transition. At death, our life timeline is the only thing we see. It displays the overall reason for our life. However, instead of having paralleled the life timeline as we approach an apex, most of us have moved further and further away from the timing. This distorts our understanding of the flow of activity and energy in the life/death system. That is why we engage in the survival fight: I don't want to go because I don't know what is going on over there; I'm at a complete loss and feel utterly impotent. There is nothing more frustrating or more fearful than that impotency at the point of death.

For the transition to life in the world hereafter, it is valuable to keep ourselves parallel with this life timeline, so that when the apex is reached, we feel at least as comfortable during this transition as we did when we were born. Death is a natural transition, a birth to the next part of the life cycle as it pertains to this particular planet.

At the actual point of death, consciousness congregates all of its energy to break free of the body. All death occurs at the connecting point at the solar plexus. It literally snaps the silver cord at the last breath. After this, the body is functionless.

The Evaluation

Once in the hereafter, the quality of the life we lived will not be determined by St. Peter at the Pearly Gates. Someone else will not be sending us to heaven or hell. Where we go in the hereafter is determined by each day we have lived, and at the end, we do our own evaluation. We are the ones who decide whether or not we did well in our life learning task. We see how our life manifested and the conduct we took on that brought us to those manifestations. At the end, you are the only one who is going to make the final judgment about yourself.

And there can be no lying. Because you'd know it was a lie, it cannot become a valid part of the story of your life. Even those greatest at denial in this life cannot lie to themselves on the other side. As we evaluate ourselves, we will all have some regret and anguish over the way we handled our life. We will see some issues that we didn't even give attention to when we were alive and wished we had created a different experience, had we known what the end result would be.

A positive and effective way to approach death is to completely embrace and fully live your life. Each of us has programmed within our cells the life learning lesson we have agreed to take on. That should be the business of each and every day. Living well means fulfilling our learning requirements. Suppose we spend a good portion of our lives helping others in kind ways. If that was not part of the learning we agreed to, when progress on the learning lesson is no longer possible, our life will end and our evaluation will turn up a lack of fulfillment. With our final breath, we will ask what we have done for and with ourselves, with the life lesson as the measure, and we will evaluate our life. This evaluation will determine the positive-negative balance of our consciousness. So live for yourself. The degree of happiness you feel in any particular moment is the degree to which you are working with the life lesson. If you think it would help, prepare an outline or a script of how you would like your life to be. You're the writer, you're the director, and you play the lead role. As for those things which are not under your control, they should be accepted as inevitable events to which you can contribute your thoughts in any way you desire. Make a plan, and consciously choose the quality of your attitude.

Your Body

Because this planet's concept is physical, even in the discarnate state we image a body. The body itself is not physical. It does not have cells and a bone structure. It exists as an image, a reflection of the body as it would be if it were physical. Whatever you see yourself to be, that is what shows up as your body. You will be the age you see yourself being, and you will be as healthy as you see yourself being. This body image can fluctuate and change during your discarnate life.

Being Met on the Other Side

Just as you are never alone in birth, you will not be alone in death. Once you have made your evaluation and determined the balance of positive-negative of the life you have just finished, you will be met. Who meets you is in part decided by your evaluation.

If you have evaluated your life (and again, you can't help but be honest) as being more negative than positive, you will be met by a discarnate worker. If you are in the lower elements of the negative condition, you probably will not respond to the worker. If you are lost in misery, you will want to stay in misery. This state is magnified in the lower negative planes, which are explained later. So you make the transition and the worker is there, but your attitude is one of disinterest. If you have fallen just under the negative-positive boundary, you may see the worker and work with this entity to create the next steps in your advancement.

If your evaluation reveals your consciousness as being more positive than negative, then it is likely you will be met by a loved one, a family member, or someone you know who has preceded you in death. It is possible that no one you know who preceded you will be available. Our loved ones who have passed on are not just over there learning to play a harp while they wait for us. They're busy and would have to be available to leave what they are doing to be there for you. If no one you knew is available, you will be met by a discarnate entity, a worker. Because you are in a positive state, you are not going to shut down to their presence as many of the negatives do.

In the Earth School there are three basic planes of discarnate existence: negative, earthbound, and positive. There are "levels" within those planes. Your evaluation will determine which plane of existence you go to next. In the following chapters, I will give an overview of what happens when your consciousness moves to the other side of the Earth School and what you can expect to see in each of these three planes of life in the hereafter.

F O U R

Overview of the Discarnate

*The chief problem about death, incidentally, is the fear that
there may be no afterlife – a depressing thought, particularly
for those who have bothered to shave. Also, there is the fear
that there is an afterlife but no one will know where it's
being held.*

—Woody Allen
Without Feathers

Your consciousness has gathered all of its energy, taken its
last breath, evaluated your life, and broken free of your
body—and you are born to the other side, the discarnate side.
It may be familiar when you get there, but whether or not it
will be delightful will depend on you. Just as there are those
here who make their life on earth a living hell and others who
seem to have found heaven on earth, so it is in the hereafter
as well. Others are there creating, working, cherishing—or
plotting, fighting, and destroying. The variations and degrees
of experience are vast, and where you will end up depends—
completely and always—on your state of consciousness.

It's mind-boggling how much you can leave behind. Just
think of not having that chain of physical life necessities
dragging on you! You may experience a magnificent feeling
of lightness as you shed your material life force and all the
responsibilities of living—paying bills, washing dishes,
shoveling snow. Movement to the discarnate is an off-loading
of a huge weight, except for those entering the negative
planes. Because those in the negative planes believe that they
still have to perform these functions, they will not experience

this off-loading, and the discarnate realm, ever responsive, contains everything necessary to continue their beliefs.

Because the Earth School is founded on physical concepts, discarnate Earth, although not made of matter, can exhibit energetic manifestations of the physical as we know it here—mountains, meadows, trees, flowers, deserts, buildings, houses, even hospitals—but they are translucent and pulsate with energy. These appearances truly are in the eye, or rather the thoughts, of the beholder.

Levels

In describing life, both here and in the hereafter, and the learning we have each taken on, it is easy to fall into thinking that we work through levels of development. The word "level" and belief in the concept of a ladder-like, upward progression in spiritual development is a pitfall of the limitations of our language. There is no ladder of progression, and there are no clear-cut levels. Yet when discussing life in the world hereafter, we often find ourselves encapsulated in a discussion about levels—levels of awareness, levels of consciousness. We begin to think that we're looking at a staircase and when each of us dies, we're at level one; then, we can move to level two and so on. Nothing could be further from the truth.

The incarnate and discarnate sides of our Earth School are maybe best represented as clusters of tightly knit spheres, like so many atoms. Within any given sphere, the positives and negatives intermix. As these spheres intermix, the variations and degrees of change and transformation are endless. Consciousness is alive and intermingling: positive-positive and negative-negative interactions and transactions; negatives transforming to positives; and positives approaching negatives. Yes, there can be a definite preponderance of positive or negative within certain spheres, however, it is not brought about by a chain of progression.

The relationship of levels to each other is the same as the relationship of one region of fog to another region of fog. If an odor in the air is created by the fog and if the wind then causes the odor to drift into another area of fog, the odor carries through. (If it's unpleasant, there will be resistance, and if it's pleasant, there will be desire.) But those in the second region are not the originators of the odor, and their experience of it is very different from the experience of those who originated it.

Another way to explain this is to imagine a see-through can containing white paint. First dribble in one color, then another. This image gives you some idea of how positive and negative can move through the mass. Sometimes they come together to blend and make an entirely new color, a whole new condition, in which negative could become more negative or negative could become more positive. Or vice versa, positive can become more negative or more positive. All variations and the degrees within them are possible.

Although when we die we do not go first to level one and move from there, I am going to present the rest of this material about the discarnate plane as if it did work that way. For the sake of being able to use this material as an informational tool, I am going to talk about the discarnate plane as if it consisted of levels, hoping you understand that the true, more comprehensive reality is an intermixed one and that when I talk about lower negatives or moving higher and closer to positive, I am not talking about levels as we typically define them.

Determining Your Entry Point into the Discarnate

Do you feel that life here is lousy but plod on, believing that once you die life on the other side will be better? Are you afraid of death? Do you wonder what happens after you die? Check in with yourself. How are you managing your life? If you had to evaluate and rate yourself right now, what percentage of you, your consciousness, would you say is positive and what percentage would you say is negative? Are you 70 percent positive and 30 percent negative? Are you 50-50? Are you 49-51? If you were to die right now, that percentage would determine where you would be positioned in the discarnate; that, and your level of fear at the moment of death.

We all have a karmic quality. This karmic quality has nothing to do with what we did for or with other people over the course of our life. When you make your transition at death, the judgment of positive-negative percentage will not be based on whether you were good to your mother, loaned your father a thousand dollars when he was destitute, kicked your dog down the stairs, or rescued a child from a burning building. *Karmic quality has to do with what you do for yourself in relation to what you came to do, your learning lesson.*

Imagine your learning lesson as a climb up a mountain, and the peak—the apex—is the full learning of that lesson. You should ask yourself, often, where you are on that mountain climb, for that will determine the positive and negative you carry within your consciousness at the moment of your transition to the discarnate world. It is only the state of our consciousness—how it totals out as an experiential result of the life—that determines where we enter the discarnate world.

We cannot go along for fifty years being a total jackass and then reverse it in one year just by doing great things, unless *we have also reversed the consciousness,* and that would involve considerable pain of awareness in which we pay karmically for those fifty rotten years. Certainly there can be an event so powerful—on a battlefield where people all around you are dying, for example—that it shatters you, disarms your established way of being, and brings you to the abrupt realization that you have been a terrible person living a terrible life. You then feel deep sorrow, guilt, and a desire to expunge the wrongs and make a profound and lasting change. But the depth of a feeling experience required to make this change is a rare occurrence. A cursory gesture of change to make something right cannot pull off an eleventh-hour save.

If your percentage of positive is below 50, the death transition will take you into either the earthbound or a negative state on the discarnate side. If your percentage is extremely negative, it will take you into the discarnate's lowest negative dimensions. The higher your percentage, the more positive your situation on the other side will be. I suspect that the greatest cause of fear at the moment of death is when people see their life as they exhale their final breath and suddenly and finally realize, "Uh-oh, this was not the accomplishment I thought it was."

With the learning lesson as the axis, the determination of your percentage is based on a multitude of variables: how you handled your life, your belief system, your hidden life, and what you think of yourself—not what others think or what so-called sins you committed but how you think of yourself. You know how you really were and how you treated life. The variables used to determine your percentage can be minute and sensitive, changing the picture a great deal.

Fear at the Moment of Death

Even if you evaluate yourself as being positive, you can still find yourself in a negative level if at the moment of death you experience great fear. You will transition to a level that directly reflects your level of fear, and because like attracts like, you will be with others who are fearful. There is a way out. On the other side, there are helpers who are committed to bringing light, truth, and understanding to individuals in dark places. If you find yourself in such a darkened place and you sense someone there with a light and they invite you to join them, you can respond to them and follow them to a different level.

The Body

Again, because this planet's concept is physical, when we die, we retain an image of a body. There is no physical body in terms of substance, but there is a body in terms of energy and sight. Just like in the incarnate, you can see other people and they can see you. The difference is that the discarnate body is an energy form and does not go through the same format and restrictions as the incarnate body. It is not weighted down by gravity. It can pass through walls. You may even think it has feeling, though it does not.

What your body will be like in the discarnate will depend on how you have been maintaining your lifestyle on that positive-negative scale. Your body's appearance will reflect how you see yourself. In some cases, people look younger, fresher, and happier after they die because of the great relief of being released from gravity and all the restrictions and requirements here—gathering food, coping with the weather, dealing with the IRS. If you transition to a positive level, eventually your body image will begin to reflect the most satisfactory age and knowledge level you had during your lifetime. For example, if you were to die at eighty-five years of age somewhat tired and stooped over, after your transition you may start showing a younger body, perhaps the body you had in your late thirties, early forties, or whatever part of your life was best and most satisfactory to you. On the other hand, if you die younger, say at fifty-five or sixty, you may not make any dramatic changes for a while, and when you do, the changes will be subtle.

If you transition to a negative level, your appearance will reflect your negative state of consciousness. Regardless of your outer appearance here, if you are a negative person, your appearance in the discarnate will precisely reflect whatever nasty state of consciousness you're holding. If you are cruel, if you look at the world as a terrible place, or if your primary attitude is one of bitterness, hatred, maliciousness, greed, hopelessness, or fear—any negative attitude—your body will conform to that primary consciousness. The greater the degree of negativity, the uglier the body image will be. Regardless of how beautiful your body may have been in the incarnate, if you spend a lifetime being hateful, your body image will look hateful.

Depending on where you fall in the positive-negative plane, you may carry some bodily desires. The more negative the state, the more you will feel the need to sleep, eat, and continue basic functions. In the positive state, you may feel a need for rest at first, and there is food provided in the form of manna if you feel the need, but these needs wane. Because there is no physical body, there are no eliminatory functions.

There are hospitals in the discarnate. That is where you will usually find negatives just moving to a positive plane or positives who were in terrible physical condition when they made the transition from the incarnate, such as after a long bout with cancer.

Sensations and Feelings

Everything is magnified in the discarnate. Without the filters of the five physical senses, colors are more intense, sound is more intense, negativity is more intense, positive actions are more intense, light is more intense, darkness is more intense, and feelings are more intense. Without the restriction of the five physical senses, your awareness of consciousness is so intense that anything that is "seen" is seen in its fundamental reality.

Vision

Everything on the incarnate plane has been redefined, redrawn, and modified from its original state. On the discarnate plane, we are free of these modifications and preconceived pictures and expectations we've carried around most of our lives. In the incarnate, for example, a man may be awed by a woman, only to be disillusioned later when he first sees her without her make-up. We redefine reality in the incarnate, but in redefining it, we also obstruct the truth of it. In the discarnate world, those in the positive states see the pure truth, beauty, and depth of each creation. There is no need to alter the original. Those in the negative states obstruct their vision, interrupting it with their predominantly negative state of consciousness. Until they change their state of consciousness, they cannot change the vision.

Sound

In making the transition, one of the first things you will be aware of, outside of the lightness of the body, is music. Not what most of us would recognize as rhythmic, the music intensifies emotions and awareness, and the interaction between you and the place you find yourself is different because of it. (In its highest form, music is used for energy propulsion and can actually move large segments of consciousness from one place to another.)

Those in the negative dimensions, because they are in such a dark, restricted space, usually will not hear it, and when they do, they do not receive it with the purity that is intended. It either frightens them because they don't know the source, or it angers them because they feel it is some kind of maneuver to take control of them. The sounds in the negative realms are screams, cries, howling, loud voices, swearing—all sounds that one might think of as coming out of angry or hateful individuals when they open their mouths.

Communicating is done through energy, the energy of being. Think of that glorious stage when a man and a woman simultaneously recognize that they love each other. There's no sound except their heartbeats, their breathing, and their energy in that micro-millisecond. Take that sensation and expand it many times over, and you get some idea of how communication occurs on the positive side.

Feelings

In the discarnate, feelings are purer. They are no longer being sifted through a series of physical strainers that modify them. You feel exactly what it is. The first feeling on the other side for someone positive making the transition is the joy that comes from throwing off the weight of the physical body and all of the things that attend to it. You don't have negative feelings and you're not emotional. Gone are all the things you've been dragging around for however many years during your incarnate experience. It is really a form of rebirth.

If you enter the negative dimensions, you feel whatever you went over with. Rage, fear, whatever negative feeling you were embracing, that is what you feel on the other side. You will also be attracted to others who've gone before you who have that same feeling. Negatives have a natural, magnetic attraction to each other. Positives do not carry this magnetic pull; they are, in a true sense, free spirits.

Darkness and Light

Darkness is not necessarily a negative in either the incarnate or the discarnate. It can be a vehicle in which you are not required to exercise attention to anything specific while you prepare to enter a different state. It becomes something that shuts out outside activity and allows you to be with just yourself, womb-like. Darkness in the positive discarnate is the same kind of darkness you experience when you're tired and curled up in your nice, warm bed with your best pillow. You close your eyes, and with all that comfort, you go to sleep. Negative darkness is a thing of horror that spawns frightful and repulsive images.

The word "light" carries different images for each of us. If we were asked to think of an apple tree, each would carry in our mind a different picture. So when we think of light, one person might think of a candle, and another would think of a flashlight beam, the light of the midday sun, or the breaking of dawn. They're all correct, but the difference in the way each light actually manifests is enormous. Light has degrees, and how it will be experienced by you in the discarnate will be according to the beliefs you formed from your lifetime experiences. If you live in the North Pole, your experience of light will be different than the experience of someone living in an equatorial region.

The vision of light is like an aperture. According to what you believe, the aperture changes to let in more or less of the light of life. Just as a camera is adjusted to let in the right amount of light to take a good picture, you do the same thing in life. The light of life you see is determined by how open your heart and soul are. The more open you are, the more of the picture you take in, and at some point, even late afternoon shadows of early darkness cannot restrict your vision.

This is not true for those who fall into the negative, who are angry or shut down. The more negative they are, the more limited their reception of light. If someone has not seen much light in his life, he may have a fear that it's going to harm him. Say, for example, he's not a good man, then light is something that threatens to expose him.

The negative person feels very dark, generally looks very dark, and believes more in the dark than in the light. Lack of vision equals lack of awareness, and lack of awareness leaves your soul in a stunted state of growth, so that when the transition occurs, you're not at all capable of dealing with the truth and beauty.

Light equals understanding, spiritually, intellectually, and physically. It's the light of self-awareness. It's hard to read a book by a match. Workers and angels on the other side work to help us see, for seeing is an illumination of the spirit. It's breathtakingly awesome. It'll knock your socks off.

Good and Evil

Before we move on to the next chapters about the positive and negative dimensions, I'd like to address the subject of good and evil, as there is a constant war that goes on between the two on both the incarnate and discarnate planes.

The Universe does not protract evil. Because the Universe is fundamentally good, we have to consider that everything working in harmony with it is working for good and that its output is good. But we can't deny the reality of evil. It exists. Wherever spirit has manifested and because free will is an inherent and integral part of the make-up of the spirit in action, we have to allow for the fact that the spirit can (and often will) make choices that in some way are not beneficial for the good of the whole. We have never had a perfect community. There have always been those who want to eat all the food, steal all the power, and enslave all the people. We're always learning about right and wrong, good and evil. And we're always in a state of freedom.

We all have the power to manifest the deepest and dearest love feelings, the kind we feel when we first fall in love with someone. It's the very thing love is supposed to be, and it can be ceaseless. Don't wait until you die to discover what life's all about. Put yourself in that place of deep, dear love, and you will remember. We should never lose sight of the fact that we are co-creators with the Universe. We have the same power as the Universe, and we can create whatever we wish. If we believe in it, we can create it. We're just a robin's feather away from using all of this unbelievable power of ours for good for ourselves, and the Universe would support us in that. There's no major threshold we have to cross to get to the Garden of Eden. We're only an inhale and exhale away.

F I V E

Below the Line
The Negative Neighborhoods

The road to hell is paved with works-in-progress.

—Philip Roth

We are all works-in-progress. Experiences present themselves to us in every moment of every day. Within the pleasure or pain, the rest or toil, the possibilities or limits of each experience, there is an opportunity for us to connect the dots of cause and effect and learn. Most of the time we do what we believe is best, based on everything we know about ourselves, our world, what we want, and the situation in which we find ourselves. We guess and we try, and if it doesn't work, we guess and try again.

We are all bound to Universal Law, and there are many ways to go about learning, some more intelligent and less painful than others. Just as we are bound to the law of gravity on Earth and ignorance of that law does not spare us from pain or even death if we jump off a building, ignorance of Universal metaphysical law does not spare us from the consequences of our choices. It stands to reason, then, that the most effective strategy for managing our lives is to develop our knowledge of how the Universe works.

There is a tremendous amount of ignorance in our Earth School, and heinous things are done. Children are brutalized, women are raped, men are murdered, races are massacred, and the planet is defiled. Yet the natural state of the Universe is one of harmony, which means every act of cruelty, carelessness, or ignorance must be balanced out. Until those responsible bear full realization of the pain and damage they have wrought, such acts commit them to steep in the darkness of what they have created. Yes, Virginia, there is a hell, and we put ourselves there.

What Makes a Negative?

What constitutes a negative? It does not necessarily take an act of monstrous evil to put us in hell. A negative does not have to be a murderer, a rapist, a thief, a liar, or an addict. He could be a parish priest, a philanthropist, a guru, or a pillar of society. He can be a spiritual leader who, in ignorance, is misleading people. So many things constitute negativity. Certainly Mr. Hitler was very negative. A hired killer is negative. But hosts of people walking around the streets today wallow in negativity: people who cheat; people who use fear and shame to manipulate others or to gain power; parents who smother their children or restrict their self-determination; businessmen and -women who would cut the insides out of their partner for money or power; people who use others only to advance themselves; people who surrender their self-determination in order to make peace; people drowning in depression; people who have truly given themselves over to despair; people who have barricaded themselves behind bitterness, spite, hostility, contempt, or self-righteousness. The variations are myriad. What constitutes a negative consciousness is nothing you and I can determine by looking at a person or his life. The negativity is related to the quality of the life experience in relationship to the learning lesson, and the lesson, when fulfilled, is always designed to be in harmony with a compassionate Universe. Someone can evangelize, sermonize, worship, meditate, abstain, or sacrifice and still be a dismal failure relative to what he has agreed to come here to do.

Our consciousness does not spontaneously change when our incarnate life ends. The condition you create for yourself here will be the condition in which you will find yourself there. That is both our saving grace and a great finger being pointed at us. The bottom line is that, in every moment, each of us is responsible for our thoughts, our acts, and our attitudes. What a great responsibility that is! But rest assured that we have at our disposal resources—books, metaphysicians, spirit guides, and our own spiritual intuition—to help us gain knowledge, understanding, wisdom, and compassion as we work on the learning we have taken on.

The Negative Planes

As I describe the conditions in the negative planes of the discarnate, bear in mind that we can continue to develop our consciousness in the hereafter, albeit in different conditions, and no one need remain stuck in any condition. We can shift to a less negative condition, to a positive one, or, of course, to a more negative state. (It is unlikely that one would slip from a positive level to a negative level while on the discarnate side of the school.)

Conditions in the negative levels range from utterly disastrous at the lowest levels to the cusp of the positive-negative line, where change can be made more easily because awareness is less blunted. I will begin by describing the lowest levels of the negative; then I will describe the higher negative range known as the earthbound plane.

Bottoming Out

In the lowest reaches of the negative planes, the intensity of the negativity overwhelms one's ability to think, evaluate, and understand. Chances are, the most negative soul will not even know that he has made the transition and is no longer incarnate. The ability of the very negative to see his surroundings logically is drastically impaired, although he does realize he is in a bad neighborhood. A discarnate worker will be there to meet and help him at the transition, but he will probably not see the worker.

The state of consciousness that is hell is not how we typically portray it—as perpetual, flesh-searing fire. No, hell is cold, bitterly cold, and damp. It is like living on a waterfront in a rat-infested cellar with heavy machinery next door grinding and pounding constantly, while above you is a Class A insane asylum. There is no relief from the relentless screaming, hollering, and bickering. The foul stench of negative dross being thrown off at an enormous rate by the souls there is inescapable. The lowest ranges are in complete darkness.

Without the filters of the physical plane, emotions are more intense, and the primary emotions in these ranges are fear, isolation, rejection, and rage. As a direct outpouring of their state of consciousness, rather than being human in appearance, negatives take on a rather animalistic appearance, and they operate within the framework of their animalistic tendencies. Senses are more intense but more intense from the negative source of themselves. Food is a need, so they manifest the need. (You can be in a very negative state as a very negative individual and still use this wonderful power of manifestation in the same way a positive person can use it to create something grand and glorious.)

There is no system of life there, no lifestyle nor life function. There is no getting along day by day, because they don't know day by day. There are no sunrises and sunsets. They have nothing to do and nothing to learn. Most of the time, they just sit.

People stay in the negative levels most often because they do not know how to get out, and they haven't the courage to find out. They find their courage—not to be confused with comfort, because nothing there is comfortable—by grouping themselves in gangs or what I call knots. Negatives have a magnetic attraction to one another. Individuals in a negative state cross into the discarnate without a sense of identity, and if they are not able to attune to the worker who meets them, they will drift toward like-negative companions. Just as in a prison, inmates who are similar in attitude, character, and condition congregate together, in the negative discarnate, knots are formed of individuals attracted to those who share their negativity — fear, misery, hatred, intolerance, rage. When this happens, they compact their negativities, producing some of the ugliest negative conditions at the lowest levels. These knots can be made up of as few as three and as many as thousands and are the worst of the conditions in the negative planes. They are held together with despair, and individuals find that they don't know how to break out of the knots and usually don't even want to. They are stuck.

One of the most dangerous jobs on the discarnate side is that of a positive discarnate worker who tries to break up these knots. The discarnate workers who volunteer to work with them must be highly skilled, because there is great danger that they, too, will get entrapped. The more negative the level, the more dangerous the work.

Earthbound

As one moves up through the negative levels, there is slowly increasing light. At the midpoint just below the positive-negative line, it is just light enough to see by, and the negativity (although still there) eases up enough so you can think a little more logically. This is the earthbound plane where you will find individuals with higher awareness but not quite yet capable of moving into the positive levels.

The transition to the earthbound plane is not as bad, and those who inhabit this state look much like they did when they passed over. Conditions here are still negative, however. It is still lonely. It is still cold but not quite as cold. It still is damp but not quite as damp. It is still noisy but not quite as noisy. It still smells bad but not quite as bad. This is a place of disappointment, disillusionment, irritation, and malaise. It is somewhat like being on the streets at nightfall in a strange country where you do not speak the language and you have nowhere to go. You are frightened.

Again, a discarnate worker will meet you but you may not care, and it is likely you will not respond. Suppose you were sitting in a room in an absolute blue funk and I came along and said, "Here, let me make you a cup of tea." How well would you respond? Probably not well at all. You would either not look at me or you would hate me for being there, because you're miserable and in no mood to be cheered up. Only in the discarnate, the intensity of that feeling is magnified. So you've made the transition and the worker is there, but your attitude is likely to be one of, so what? Things are the way that they are, and you've ended up where you expected to end up.

This is where most of us enter the discarnate side of the school. Reasons for making the transition into these not-quite-positive ranges are numerous, although again, the primary cause is ignorance—ignorance of the Universe, of law, of function. Here you will find the overindulger—the overeater, the minor but real alcoholic, the person with a negative attitude, the misguided religious type—anything that is negative but not grossly so. Resentment, even if it seems justified, can put you here. Many who have died violently—in a war, earthquake, or typhoon—and are caught up in the negativity and fear of the situation, end up here.

The earthbound state is a kind of limbo, and getting out requires a turning of the consciousness away from a negative condition and toward a positive one. There will always be a worker there to help you, if you will only see and respond.

What We Can Do Now

Although few of us expect we will, as things stand now, most of us will end up below the positive-negative line. Someone once asked Americans to rate themselves as drivers: below-average, average, or above-average. Almost 90 percent of the people reported themselves as being above-average. Yet each year over, there are six million police-reported vehicle accidents in the United States, with over one-third resulting in injury. This doesn't even begin to count parking lot fender-benders and other unreported accidents. At this point of our incarnate life, perhaps our self-assessment is not as accurate as we think.

As we go about the experience of living, we should be aware of two issues: The primary one is the ongoing development of our spirit into positive experiences. The secondary issue is how we contribute to humanity — are we putting out a positive attitude?

When you are in difficult situations, ask yourself what your life is trying to show you. Explore how you can change your attitude and perspective so that when frustrations, difficulties, and hard times fall upon you, you can turn them into something that works for you in a positive direction. You can also ask yourself to assess how comfortable you really are being positive, especially in a culture where it is considered socially sophisticated and adroit to be negative. If you cannot be comfortable being in a positive state here, then you cannot transition to a positive state in the discarnate.

Being positive is a matter of discipline. As well as learning how the universe works, we must continually develop our self-awareness. For example, take the all-too-common and inconvenient computer virus. It is one those things that happens on this plane, and we'd all be better off if we didn't magnify it into a personal issue. Don't let yourself feel like a victim. Don't let yourself get caught up in anger at whoever created the virus. Just take care of business. And if it still feels personal and you still feel punished, attacked, or angry, ask yourself what this experience is offering to teach you about yourself.

What about those who are already in the negative discarnate planes? It's tempting to forget about them and let them stew in their own mess, especially those who have hurt us deeply with their legacy of hate, cruelty, and stupidity. But in the Earth School, incarnate and discarnate are bound to each other for as long this planet shall exist. So ditching the negatives is not an option. Not only that, but there are people in the earthbound and negative planes who have been there since the very beginning of mankind, and the population of the negative discarnate is now enormous. The entire population on Earth today as compared to the population in the negative discarnate is like the size of a lake as compared to the ocean. This is why we have not made significant progress in our overall development. We've got such enormous negative feedback passing through that it is easy to fall in with it, and every time we are mad or upset, even at the smallest thing, it becomes part and parcel of that ocean of negativity.

What can we do? First, we must examine ourselves and shift our attitude so that we receive our experiences with enthusiasm and respect. We must change our perspective of difficulties, see them as opportunities, and act only with integrity. As George Bernard Shaw said, "Life isn't about finding yourself. Life is about creating yourself."

On a societal level, there are many things we can do. Whenever we take the life of another — by electric chair, in the gas chamber, on the battlefield, or in any of the other ways we terminate the life of another — we fuel negativity by igniting the rage, stoking the fear, and corroborating despair. For many hundreds of years, we have been creating and removing negatives from the incarnate at a rate much greater than we have been creating positives. As long as we continue to do this, even when it's to legally execute a murderer, more negatives will continue to reincarnate. They have to come back, for they have a growth experience to complete here. At some point, even if it is later and in a reconstituted state, we will have to deal with them. We must find ways to contain their damage and encourage their learning without taking their lives.

Almost all of the war death population is going to end up below the positive-negative line. Perhaps one of the most profound changes we can make to is to stop war.

Finally, strive to put yourself into the world in positive ways. Let's make that the socially adroit way of being.

The opposite of good is not evil. The opposite of good is ignorance. And, in this compassionate Universe in which harmony and balance ultimately rule, the lessons will be learned.

Above the Line
The Positive Neighborhoods

*Men are admitted into Heaven not because they have curbed
& govern'd their Passions or have no Passions, but because
they have Cultivated their Understandings. The Treasures
of Heaven are not Negations of Passion, but Realities of
Intellect, from which all the Passions Emanate Uncurbed in
their Eternal Glory. The fool shall not enter Heaven. Let him
be ever so holy.*

— William Blake
A Vision of the Last Judgement

Most of us believe that if we've led a good and honorable life,
we'll go to heaven — Paradise, the Garden of Eden, the
Elysian Fields, Valhalla, the Isle of Avalon, the state of
Nirvana, the happy hunting grounds — some place where we
will be eternally rewarded, a place where the donkey finally
catches up with the carrot. No more struggling, no more pain,
no more lack, and best of all, no more trying to figure it all
out, because the answers will be there waiting for us. It's not
quite that way. Although it is a place of light and harmony,
as in the incarnate world, the experiences and learning
continue in the positive discarnate world of this dual-sided
Earth School.

If we are looking to reap reward, we must develop our
knowledge of how the Universe works and use that
knowledge to expand our own quality as human beings and
to live fully. We begin to develop that knowledge by

accepting complete responsibility for ourselves and the lives we're leading. No one else is responsible for our pain, our suffering, or whether or not we experience joy and fulfillment. Those are generated and sustained by our thought-responses. If we take responsibility for ourselves; if we pay attention to the laws of cause and effect, developing our knowledge of them and consciously working to improve our personal quality; and if we have a basically good attitude, then unless something goes amiss in the death transition (such as a violent death that causes disorientation and fear, which must be broken through first), we will end up in the positive discarnate plane.

As we review the conditions of the positive transition and life on the positive plane, please remember that there are a multitude of variations. I have chosen something of a logical norm to discuss, and what I describe here is a limited explanation. We will begin with the just-above-the-line experience.

Lightness of Being

The first thing many new discarnates notice is the light. It is not a kind of light we understand here. It is not like sunlight or light-bulb light. The etheric light is without shadow, and everything is filled with it. It soothes, calms, and energizes.

You will feel a great sense of relief at no longer being burdened with the responsibilities of the physical plane. There are no bills to pay, no food to buy, no time clock to punch. The attitude of consciousness moving into the positive transition is optimistic. There is a sense that this is great, and you're really glad to be here. Unlike those who fall into the negative and earthbound planes, you know that you're dead and in a different place. You're glad because, chances are, you died through illness, accident, or some other painful circumstance, and where you are now feels a whole lot better than just before the transition. You really have no intention of turning around and going back, because this feels just fine.

You retain a body image, and unless you were ill for a long time before your death, your body image will reflect the age that was the most satisfying to you in life. You are no longer bound by gravity or the physical laws of the incarnate world, so your body image is not weighted down. It can walk through walls. You may even think it has sensation, although it doesn't. Unlike the negatives or the earthbound, you will not feel a desire to get back into the physical body.

The transition to the positive is a clean jump that places you in a mode of immediate acceptance and relief, and it's marvelous.

Being Met

In the transition to the discarnate, it can be difficult to recognize where you are. So you will most likely be met by someone you know, a family member or friend who preceded you in death. This person will draw your focus, and your recognition of him or her helps your orientation. In rare cases, no one who preceded the dying person is available. (They have responsibilities on the other side as well.) If this happens, you will be met by a discarnate entity, a worker. Unlike most of the negatives, you will not shut down and ignore the entity. Because you're in a positive state, you will see this worker.

Hospitals

Some positives make the transition, meet with a family member or friend to get oriented, and then go right into a hospital on the other side. It may be surprising that there would be a need for a hospital when there is no physical body. But we do have a consciousness, and it may need to be restored, as certain experiences can considerably impair our level of energy so that consciousness cannot function on its own. People who end up in hospitals are those who have been badly mangled, extremely ill, or very negative and taken out of below-the-line experiences by discarnate workers. How long any individual stays depends on the condition of the consciousness. It can take anywhere from months to thousands of years. For example, if a person just came out of a negative knot, he would not be reincarnated right away but sent to the hospital to restore a semblance of balance to his consciousness. Because of the severe conditions in a negative knot, that can take more than a thousand years of earth time. Long bouts of cancer, long-term illness, and the fever diseases are all terribly debilitating to the consciousness. People who died of these causes are likely to be hospitalized for many months, if not for a few years. The purpose of hospitals in the discarnate is to restore the consciousness to the point that it can reestablish a body image.

Discarnate hospitals function similarly to those in the incarnate, except that there is no lack of resources and no proof of insurance needed. The first person to see you, and who has a great deal of control of over what is being done to you, is not the doctor but the karmic technician. He shows up, and he immediately understands the karmic pattern from the incarnate, the karmic pattern from the discarnate, and the damage in the consciousness relative to the damage in the karmic pattern. He advises the doctors as to what is needed. The doctors take over and prescribe the proper energy patterns, energy infusions, color infusions, reflective infusions, sound, triangulations, and all that is necessary to restore the consciousness. Nurses are there to carry out the treatment to restore the consciousness to its primary karmic balance — that is, the balance of knowing, the balance of will, and the balance to be able to function.

Birthing Area

The level that I will describe now is where you make the
transition if you are in a fairly healthy state of consciousness
and do not require hospitalization. Also, those who have
completed their rebalancing in the hospital may move on to
this level. I have chosen to describe this level because it is
where the greatest number of positives spend much of their
discarnate time. Everything at this level is designed to help
new discarnates acclimate to the change.

Fairly soon after your transition and after you have had a
reunion with the person who has met you, he or she will take
you to a guide teacher. Your family member or friend will
then leave. The guide teacher will show you where you're
going to live. There is a street where you will live and a
house. The house is not furnished with your things, but it is
furnished comfortably. Of course, these are all things we
don't need, but most of us think we do, at least at this level.
Usually there is food there, although I can guarantee you it's
not going to be lamb chops or pork chops but primarily fruit
and some liquid, which you may or may not want to eat. It is
not necessary for you to eat, and there is no eliminatory
function, but you may eat if you wish. The food is in the
nature of manna, spiritual nourishment, and eating it is like
ingesting a form of energy that not only helps sustain your
energy but helps you see more clearly the condition you're in
and adapt to the change more harmoniously.

There is a great desire, immediately after you get there, to
sleep. You are tired, very, very tired. The guide teacher
suggests you lie down and rest, and he or she will come and
get you after you have had a good sleep. You are not
lonesome but peaceful. It is like sneaking off to an afternoon
nap without guilt or pressure. Everything is quiet (no
phones), and the kids are happy and busy elsewhere. It's that
kind of a rest, a rest that brings you back to sweet childhood
naps, only better. You get that delicious, complete feeling that

everything is perfect, nothing is wrong, and there is nothing you have to do. The consciousness just sops up all that energy and rebalancing. In earth time, that sleep can last a couple of days, a couple of weeks, a few months, or at most, a year.

When you awake, you know that you're dead, but not having body weight and the fact that things here are just plain different can be a bit disorienting. The guide teacher, aware of this, will be there to take you on a tour of where you are, to help you get oriented and to answer your questions.

You'll see that the buildings are not solid but translucent and pulsating with energy. At some point you'll realize that you've been traveling around, but you haven't been walking or riding in a car, a train, or even upon a cloud. You've been moving via thought transfer—you think about where you want to go, and with no wind, no transition, you'll just be there.

The desire to turn around and go back to the incarnate side of the school is practically nil, other than maybe wanting to take a quick look. Most people do ask about the family they left behind. If you're in a fairly healthy state, they will ask if you want to see them. If you say yes, your guide or another worker will take you to the edges of the energy line and let you view your family. Often the person will see his family crying and wailing or quarreling over money and property and, in general, just not doing what he'd hoped. It can be a distasteful experience, although most want to do it. But you don't have to.

Creativity and Entertainment

Your guide will show you what activities are taking place and what kind of work is being done. At this level, you can choose involvement in a creative effort and/or entertainment.

The creative efforts are simple, and people pursue the creative activities that interest them. There are artists, painters, sculptors, and people working in metal and cloth. There are musicians playing and people working in gardens. There are people working with weaving, food creation, and things of the sea. (Yes, there are seas there.) There are no limits. No one there works at a job. No one is digging ditches, laying sewer lines, cleaning house, or polishing silver. You might find someone like a shoemaker, for example, but it will be a creative pursuit, not work. He may be making lovely, shiny-gold boots out of energy.

Your guide knows you well, knows how you function and what you want, and eventually will offer you the creative element that suits you and gives you an opportunity to develop your creative talent. Restoration occurs in the creative process itself, especially in knowing that you are creative and discovering that you can do all these things you didn't know you were capable of. It's not the mundane experience of picking up a paintbrush, dipping it into a pot, and putting it on a canvas. It's taking energy and remolding it into form, much like sculpturing. Or it's turning energy into colors with a sweep of a hand moving through a level of energy and wiping purity of color onto a space. That you can do this is exhilarating and exciting. It's like the energized feeling you get here when you're involved in something you're passionate about, only better. The new discarnate, free from dealing with the weight of the body and the structure of the physical world, finds there are all these things he didn't know he could be involved in—energy, color, music. This awareness, probably unavailable to him in the incarnate world, is absolutely thrilling, and he feels much like a kid in the toy store after hours—there are all these things to play with.

One of the more frustrating things I come across is when I ask someone what he or she does creatively, and the answer is, "Nothing. I'm just not a creative person." Thinking that you're not creative is a denial that does not set well when you get to the discarnate, and you have a good chance of ending up just below the line because you don't want to be who you really are; you don't want to use your talent and create. Creativity and its expression are basic to our nature. Everyone is creative. So if you find yourself thinking that you're not creative, especially at the moment of transition, you can be fairly sure you will not end up on a positive plane.

In addition to creative opportunities, you will find entertainment. You may either participate or just enjoy listening and watching. Entertainment provides healing and restoration for the consciousness, which at this level must adjust to the change of vibration and be content and happy. The two primary entertainments are music and dancing/marching. Here, marching is a form of dancing where everyone moves together in harmony and balance. At this heightened level of sensation, the music is beyond what we can hear in the incarnate. It has a depth that moves through you and becomes a part of you.

Now this level is sweet and maybe a bit corny sounding, but bear in mind that you are a baby in the discarnate world. We don't put babies to work when they're born here. The first things we do are to feed them, let them sleep, hug them, kiss them, nurture them, and teach them to play. We put bright things in their cribs and encourage them to do what they enjoy. For most positives, the entry into the discarnate is analogous to birth in the incarnate, except the consciousness is at a more aware level. While not exactly the infancy we know here, it is still a form of infancy. That is why this level is designed to be basic and easy. This is where the majority of positives go when they enter the discarnate. If this elementary level would bore you, then you would go to a higher level.

Moving Up

There are individuals who make enormous jumps into higher levels once they make the transition into the discarnate. On the high planes, they do not evidence a body. Individuals who transition here are those who came to do mission work on the planet, and they return to the higher level from which they came and move on from there. Beings here are light forms, and light forms can be anything they want to be and morph into anything they like—butterflies, people, whatever they desire.

In these levels, the fundamentals of energy use and how energy works under various formats are learned. Here is where you can think a thought and produce an energy form equal to that thought. You think a butterfly and then you think the colors. Then you can, if you wish to think it, morph that butterfly into dragon or fantasy animal. It is fascinating that you can produce what you think, and you recognize that you are part of the co-creative process and can co-create in an enormous way that is awesome and exciting. That's just a basic level.

On yet higher planes, you learn how to use energy as life form. You can create a seed and actually make that seed go through the levels of its growth right in front of your eyes— the seed sprouts, becomes a plant, then a bush, then it flowers. You can do this on any scale. You can make a forest or a waterfall. This is like playtime and it's learning. The object, once again, is to get you oriented and show you what you're capable of doing, because individuals eventually move on to be part of the hierarchy and administration that oversees the incarnate world.

Work in the Discarnate

Work in the discarnate is an activity that fits your unique talent and creativity. It is fulfilling and pleasing. Everyone has a unique individual quality. Like an orchestra where violins are not playing trumpet scores and trumpets are not playing flute scores, each of us is an instrument and we play our own score, one we thrill to, and it is in magnificent harmony beyond anything we know here.

Because this is a dual-sided school where the discarnate and incarnate reflect each other, you will see many resemblances in the way things are run in the discarnate, although at a higher level of awareness. There are basic administration jobs tantamount to operating a government or corporation here, and there is a need for people to keep records and run the various operations by overseeing and directing them. There are workers who care for those whose consciousness has been impaired in the incarnate. There are also workers who manufacture clothing and produce food. Others are etheric soldiers, karmic technicians, and more. We'll review a few types of workers.

Discarnate Transition Workers

These are the workers who meet entities making the transition from the incarnate. They are also there during a mass catastrophe, like an earthquake or a typhoon, when there may be thousands of souls making the transition all at once. These workers have to know a great deal about how consciousness reacts in the transition, what each lacks, and how to fill that need. Consciousness has a wide range of reactions. Confusion, however, seems to be the greatest problem. *Where am I? Why am I leaving and why should I leave the physical plane that I'm used to and go into the discarnate plane?* This worker has to have the ability to hold the consciousness at a point where enough recognition is established to get it to move properly through the transition phase. It's like a newborn baby here who starts crying. You would not stand over him and scream, "Stop it!" He would only cry more because you have frightened him, to say nothing of having telepathically induced him with all that negative energy. The same condition exists in the transition to the discarnate. Whether it's a mass transition or a very difficult transition, we can't say to the consciousness, Okay, you're dead now, so come with me and we'll take care of everything. Consciousness is crying. It's confused, and it doesn't know what to do or where to go. It's a bit frightened and off balance. It needs the tenderness, understanding, and empathy of the worker who holds it, takes care of it, moves it along carefully, and understands what it needs in the way of the transitional energy so as not to lose it to a below-the-line experience. It takes technical training to know how to do this.

Clothing Production

People in the incarnate do not run around naked, so entities in the discarnate do not run around naked. Clothing there is translucent in nature, and although everyone there could manifest their own clothes if they wanted to, there is clothing production for those who wish to create clothing. There are no factories or mechanical devices in the discarnate, and the clothing is not sewn as it is here. The work is done in a place more like a beautiful resort, and the production is etheric. The workers extend their consciousness energy out beyond a finger, like an energy needle. Then, they reach out and clip off a strand of energy, pull it, transfer it to the other hand, and catch another one. No tools are needed, because their own energy pattern is the tool that weaves these tremendous energy strands like hot silver or gold threads. As they weave, the strands expand. The energy coming in for them to work with makes a sound like the clinking of millions of high-sounding bells or fluid diamonds falling gently over a waterfall.

Food Production

A similar system works out in the field with food workers learning to make food from manna. A group works with a higher technician whose ability is above theirs. He produces an etheric seed and puts the seed in the center of the circle of workers. The workers then project and extend their energy, and immediately a system begins — roots, stalk, tree, leaves, blossoms. The entire thing grows in a matter seconds — minutes at the most. Then the fruit appears. They harvest it and take it back. When the fruit has been harvested, the tree is then put back into its original energy form, because it has fulfilled its cycle. Harmonious music is a part of this process as well.

Higher Level Work

As part of your experience here sooner or later (and it can take millions of years), you will reach a point, higher in the levels, where you will take on responsibility for some part of the incarnate world. You will administer the positive activity of this planet and the people on it without interfering with free will. You will also be combating — if that's the right word — the forces of negativity. There is an entire world of discarnates in the place we call hell, and keeping them from infecting the incarnate world with their plague of negativity is a big-time job. A good part of the positive discarnate work is to express power to keep the negative from becoming rampant and turning this whole planet into a mass of negative chaos.

There are many levels of work in the positive discarnate, some of which are quite technical and require training and knowledge to work with energies. You can become a karmic technician or someone who works with the negative plane. There are also areas not immediately connected with the activity of incarnate Earth: Earth karmic patterns and road making, for example.

Karmic Technician. Karma is the Law of Cause and Effect. Every cause produces an effect, and absolutely nothing can occur outside the Law of Karma. A karmic technician is an expert in karma. Among them are the workers who go down into negative areas to try to rescue consciousnesses or break up knots. They must be highly trained and exceedingly skilled in working with energies.

Earth Karma Worker. This is an area not immediately connected with the activity of individuals on the Earth. Those working in this area are concerned with the karmic patterns that Earth itself is establishing. They work with pattern responses to major events, such as wars and natural catastrophes. This is highly technical work involving the transfer of energies to maintain magnetic balance on the planet. These workers cannot interfere with our free will, so if we're going to do all these stupid things, they have to work like crazy trying to keep the Earth level balanced so that we don't destroy ourselves. Any destruction on the Earth has an enormous effect in the discarnate area as well.

Etheric Soldier. The battle of good and evil is specific to the Earth School, and in order to teach the range of lessons it's supposed to, there must be both. The negative forces that try to disrupt and destroy the positive forces come from hell, that area where the negative consciousnesses join together in producing their own leaders and their own hierarchy. However you wish to think of them—the devil and his forces, false prophets, or negative angels—they, too, work on two planes: (1) to influence the negatives in the incarnate and make them more negative and (2) to use their negative power to overcome the positive power in the etheric planes. Etheric soldiers deal with negative forces on an etheric level. This battle is enormous and never-ending, and the good guys need soldier technicians to set up the proper conditions to prevent this negative force from overtaking the school.

Evil is formulated out of the same creative reality that good is. The only difference between a god and a devil is the intent when using creative power. Evil is really ignorance. Good is knowledge. Those who perpetuate evil use exactly the same power, the same energy, as those who perpetuate good, but they use it in ignorance to destroy instead of with intelligence to produce creatively. Those who do evil believe in what they're doing, as do those who do good. We can choose where we wish to stand by looking at their results. Evil results in repetitious patterns of pain and destruction. Good results in new experiences of happiness and harmony.

Evil cannot be destroyed, but it can be transformed at its source. When you get to the level of being able to work as an etheric soldier, you must know about energy and energy splitting. In splitting energy, you reduce its effectiveness. It's like watering down gasoline. Adding just a little water to gasoline wouldn't change anything, adding a little more would make the car ping, a little more would make it chug, and a little more would make it ineffectual. Energy splitting works the same way: By adding elements that are incompatible with the energy itself, we dissipate its quality and it becomes ineffective.

I've been asked whether it interferes with the free will of the negatives if we go in to split the energy. No, it doesn't. Free will is an aspect only of good. Evil (i.e., ignorance) nullifies free will; the more ignorant, the less free. Ignorance impairs the flow of free will.

Road Makers. An area of highly technical work that I particularly like is etheric road making. This is also upper level work, as road makers must understand how everything in space moves on both the physical and etheric planes. Every star, every planet, every moon, every asteroid, every solar system, and every galaxy is moving, and they pass each other. They're not bouncing around like pinballs and banging into each other because there are workers keeping all those bodies in their proper orbit as they move and pass one another. Their collision, or even near-misses of their energy fields, would release an utterly destructive force. Road makers are responsible for developing energy pathways for each celestial body and galaxy so they don't collide. The road makers must anticipate the cyclic timing of all these constantly moving bodies, and they cannot afford to be off by one fractional iota of that cycle. Etheric road makers must have a highly developed understanding of energy, its frequencies, and how to lay out the energy of each celestial body in the universe. There are crossroads, interchanges, and intricate networks of overpasses and underpasses we haven't even imagined yet on the incarnate.

Relationships on the Positive Plane

Relationships in the positive discarnate are quite different. They are characterized by individuality, cooperation, and harmony. No longer burdened by the distractions of making a living, attending obligatory social functions, or watching TV and no longer encumbered by expectations and capricious emotions, relationships finally know harmony and joy. It is a coming into one another's presence fully conscious and without barriers. It is real love … and it is truly breathtaking.

Relationships between men and women on the positive discarnate are terrific. Gone are the limiting and mundane terms we apply here. There, relationships are a pure love interchange. There is also a sexual interchange but not as we know it here. The love-sex feelings are an exquisite union of pure energy.

What about meeting up with Aunt Tilly or Mom or your first husband? If you want to meet up with someone who preceded you in death, you probably will, if he or she is available. Again, they're not just on the other side waiting for us, but they're doing some kind of work or fulfilling a learning requirement. It's also possible that this person may have already reincarnated.

It does happen that discarnates who have died before us oversee us while we're still in the incarnate, such as a mother who has died and watches over her son from the other side. If she's doing it in full awareness that she herself has a responsibility to move onward and knows that at the right time she'll go, that's a positive thing. If she's doing it out of emotional pull, that's negative, and it's likely she's acting from the earthbound plane not the positive plane. It should be clear which plane the discarnate is acting from by the quality of the overseeing and the help that comes through to us.

The Earth Hierarchy

The Universe has organization and an operational system. Without hierarchy, we would have chaos. Although chaos is available on the negative plane, the Universe itself is not chaotic.

Here is how the Earth hierarchy is laid out: Let's begin with you, a single incarnated individual. Attached to you is a discarnate band usually made up of five individuals who oversee and impress you to do the right—or harmonious— thing. It can be more than five, but five is most common. Above that band is a group of teachers, which is the administrative level. Above the teachers is a council. The council is usually comprised of twelve to fifteen individuals. For a planet this size, there are hundreds of councils. Above the councils are masters, of which there are three for Earth, and this number changes as the population changes. Above the masters, there is the avatar. The avatar is what we think of as God. The avatar is responsible for the planet and obviously has lots of help.

That's the basic construction of our Earth hierarchy. There are hierarchies above ours as well. The Universe operates within an intelligent, well organized, well run system for the production of good.

When you find yourself working within the positive discarnate hierarchy, you will see no back biting, you will not feel a need to compete, and you will feel no jealousy over someone holding a higher position than you. It is harmonious, and everyone is delighted with whatever part they're involved in because they're getting so much from it. It wouldn't occur to anyone to think he or she was lesser than someone else. There is no lesser. It would be out of context. Besides, everyone has plenty to do.

Reincarnation

People have asked why we would bother returning to the incarnate plane if things are so wonderful in the positive discarnate. My answer is that we are here completing the life cycle picture. If we didn't return to the incarnate plane, we'd have only half the picture in this two-sided school.

At some point in the discarnate experience, from within you comes an awareness that it is important to come back and continue the incarnate experience and education. When you realize this, you make it known to your higher guide on the discarnate. The guide arranges for you to appear before the Reincarnation Board. The Reincarnation Board is made up of anywhere from five to fifteen individuals of considerable ability and knowledge. You tell them that you would like to go back and continue your experience and learning process on the incarnate level. The board says fine and asks you to reappear after they have laid out a blueprint of your next incarnated life. Like the blueprint of a building, which shows only the construction and not the colors of the walls or the type of furniture, this blueprint shows only the structure of the life, not the details. This is an important point. It's a blueprint of what the incarnate life is for and what it is to be like in order to fulfill your requirements for advancement. It includes information about the type of parents you will have (although not the specific people) and the type of life you will be born into. It also shows where the development of the planet will be where you reincarnate. You're given a lot of information, and because you realize that it is what you need and should be doing, you can sign off on it.

Once you have agreed to take on the life, you are put in a different space, a holding pattern, where your energy level can be reduced. It has to be, otherwise you could not inhabit a physical body with the intensity you have as a discarnate being. Your energy level is toned down bit by bit so you can match a physical body as a baby in the incarnating process.

After the holding space, you move to a new space where you become aware of the fetus in the mother you'll be born to. Pregnant women often relate that during their pregnancy they could actually feel the presence of the child walking next to them. But you're not actually in that body yet. During the time that that mother is pregnant and carrying that fetus, all the cells and all the history are completely her. It is when the baby is delivered and the first breath is taken that your consciousness slams into that body, pushing out the cells containing the history of the mother as you take over the vehicle. That process is physically painful and is one of the reasons that babies cry, but it lasts only microseconds. Then, there you are, a new baby, a new consciousness, all of your characteristics now in this body and ready to operate on the incarnate plane.

Karmic Balance

Eventually, in order to graduate from this school, we have to reach a point of balance. That balance is attained when the incarnate and discarnate worlds come together for us as one unit, and we can easily walk through both worlds at will without obstruction. To do this, karma must be balanced on both sides and the information from both brought together into a coordinated point where you can see as a complete unit the experience=awareness=knowledge=wisdom™ gathered by the two separate means. We end up with the triangle again. The trilogy, the trinity, by whatever name we call it, it is a three-pointed condition: We take the discarnate karma and the incarnate karma, which are the learning experiences, and put them together into the third, which is completeness. We become who we were intended to be.

Each of us has agreed to come here to develop an enormity of knowledge. When we graduate from here, we will take with us out into the universe a depth of awareness, profound compassion, and mastery of our co-creative skill. Then, in our never-ending pursuit for the answer, we will embark on new experiences elsewhere in the universe. Yet the answers we get will give us more questions, which will need more answers, and on it goes. When we do catch the carrot, there is always another dangling in front of us, and we'd have it no other way.

SEVEN

Astral Rescue Work

I have lost friends, some by death ... others through sheer inability to cross the street.

—Virginia Woolf

Who wouldn't want life in the hereafter to be an easy sail through a tunnel of light that takes us to a port of bliss? Yet the act of dying itself cannot send us to a world of light and love. It cannot purge us of our sorrows, fear, hatred, resentment, or ignorance. It is only our state of mind, body, and soul at the moment of death that determines where we make port in the afterlife.

If we have cultivated negativity in our life or if we get entangled in negativity at the moment of death, we will begin the afterlife in the negative planes. Then, in death as in life, our condition can change only when we make a conscious choice and take action to support that choice. In terms of negativity, that choice and those actions would be to expose our fear, release our negativity, and accept that there is more to this experience than we have yet seen, an intelligence and goodness far beyond our ability to imagine. This is easier for some than for others.

In Tibet, I was trained by the sages in esoteric arts and disciplines, including the development and honing of my clairvoyant abilities. In addition to doing life readings, I used what I had learned to work with souls in the afterlife who were ensnared in their own negativity. In the 1960s, at the request of a researcher of the paranormal, a team was formed to create a record of the astral rescue work. The cases told of here come from that time.

Many individuals and groups around the world have done spiritual rescue work using various methods and formats. What was different about how our team worked was that we concentrated over a specific period of time; whereas, others had done this work on a sporadic basis with few, if any, keeping complete records. Any astral rescue work is valuable, but because we kept meticulous records of the "conversations" with the discarnates, we were able to compile something of a spiritual journal. Conditions of our world being what they are, I believe most of us will begin our life after death in this negative, earthbound state. So I wish to describe some of the work done with those souls—how they came to be where they were and what helped them to release their negativity and move on. Experience is the best teacher, and our contacts were in the been-there-done-that position.

Again, where we embark on our journey after we die depends entirely upon our state of consciousness at the time of death and its positive-negative balance. If we are more negative than positive, we will begin our life in the hereafter in the negative planes of the discarnate realm. The upper reaches of those planes are what I refer to here as the earthbound planes. It is here where we find souls who died while bearing a milder condition of negativity—addictions of any sort, mild depression, a disagreeable temperament, and especially those who experienced a traumatic death. Almost everyone who experiences a death by trauma—car accident, plane crash, train crash, weather-related disaster, victims of murder, and especially those who die in war—will end up in the earthbound plane, at least for a time.[4] Once the negative

---

[4] As for the rest, those rare individuals who can maintain a positive consciousness even in the face of this type of death move right through the earthbound and on to the positive levels. Those who

energy of the consciousness is released, these souls can move on, rest, obtain more comprehensive healing, or go to work.

Judging from the condition of the world in the last hundred years alone, the total number of souls starting their latest discarnate experience in the earthbound must be tremendous. In the twentieth century, the deadliest earthquakes—classified as those that kill more than 50,000—caused the deaths of well over a million people. Even if we used a liberal estimate that only 50 percent of those souls ended up in the earthbound, the result is a half-million. Add to that the traumatic deaths from World War I, World War II, the Korean War, the Vietnam War, the massacres and ethnic cleansings in Russia, Europe, and Africa, and all the other natural disasters in the world—floods, cyclones, hurricanes—and divide it by half (again, in my opinion, a generously low figure considering the fear and confusion involved in a traumatic death), and we can reasonably conclude that the population in the earthbound has skyrocketed.

Each of the numerous levels, or planes, (actually, they're more like neighborhoods) of the afterlife is populated by souls who share a common belief structure. The negative person who had little or no positive view of life on earth and manifested that negativity in his daily habits would make his entrance into the discarnate on a plane with like-minded souls. The unbreakable rule is like attracts like.

The conditions as they normally are in the discarnate plane can be likened to any large city almost anywhere in the world. Every city has its upper-class inhabitants, usually found in spacious homes on expansive grounds where living is pleasant, genteel, and fulfilling. The people who inhabit these areas are, for the most part, educated and conscious of their responsibility to their community and to humanity in

---

embrace a deeper level of negative consciousness will, of course, move to the lower-negative planes.

general. If we were to transpose this community to the etheric plane, we would find it situated in an area of light, an awakened plane of spiritual consciousness, responsibility, and service. Of course, cities encompass other areas that range from middle class to slums inhabited by people with varying degrees of education and consciousness, and they express themselves accordingly. In the most poverty-stricken areas, you will find dirt and darkness, hate and despair, fear and chicanery. For each individual, the condition is the same as it was on Earth. It does not change simply because one has moved from the incarnate to the discarnate.

Another aspect of the earthbound neighborhoods of the afterlife is that all sense of time is lost almost immediately. Incarnate time is incarnate time; it does not follow in the earthbound. In the earthbound, there are no days, weeks, or months. No sunrises and sunsets. So when we asked the earthbound subjects we worked with when they were born, they usually didn't know. I remember one of the older subjects we worked with was a Spanish man killed back in the fifteen hundreds, as best we could gather. We had a terrible time getting dates out of him. His range of dates spanned a four-hundred-year period, and it really didn't make any difference to him. He couldn't conceive what four hundred years was, so he was giving us any date that came into his mind.

The next thing to go for earthbounds is their name. One of the more amusing aspects of dealing with them was that they gave us any name they wanted. Even though we soon realized that they were right only occasionally, we continued to ask for their name so we could keep them focused. For instance, when asking a name, I might get "Alice Smith." But because I was able to see her pattern—a radiation of energy every one of us has—I could see that that wasn't true. So I would say, "Well, I don't think that's your name. What is your name?"

"Uh, Mary Jones."

"That's not your name, either. What is your name?"

"Uh, Alice Carpenter." And it would go on like that.

One time, a subject gave a name that was so ridiculous that I asked, "Where in the world did you get that name?"

The subject replied, "Someone out there [in the earthbound neighborhood] was yelling it to me." Things can get pretty confusing at that level.

Earthbound is a most unhappy place, comprised, as are all levels, of the totality of the consciousness of its occupants. The good news is that it takes only the slightest nudge to an individual's consciousness to catapult him into the brilliant afterlife of the positive planes. That was our hope for and intent with each soul we worked with.

The Team

My role was as a clairvoyant, able to "see" and communicate with those on the discarnate side of the Earth School. Other members of the team included someone who served as a channel and wrote the responses of the earthbound subjects; someone who kept records of the sessions, recording me speaking aloud as I addressed the discarnate subjects and making a record of the channel's writing; and finally, the researcher of the paranormal. Occasionally visitors came to see what it was all about.

The team was comprised of, not only those of us on the incarnate plane, but of members on the discarnate plane as well—those who were familiar with the issues of discarnate life. The most significant member was our primary discarnate contact, a highly evolved spiritual consciousness who was an expert facilitator on the astral plane. It is enough for our purposes here to refer to him as "X," as indeed this was the letter his name began with. His consciousness was of such spiritual magnitude and power that no force of negation born on the earth plane could overcome it—a quality vital to the safety of all involved. "X" also channeled tremendous heavenly power that could be focused on the subject whose awareness we were trying to help recharge and magnify so he could realize both the position he was in and the opportunity to change being set before him.

But we learned that still more help was needed: A group, unknown to us until the work had progressed to some degree, revealed itself to us. We termed them the "advance men." Sometimes, the situation would be so peculiar, the individual so difficult, or our need for information so much greater than the subject had access to that these advance men would step in with the help we needed. Without their preparation on the discarnate side, the work could not have been done successfully. Being in the incarnate, we had built-in limitations when trying to read the energy patterns on the other side. Even as capable as I was at this, I could have easily made errors in judgment as to how able and competent the subject was. This advance intelligence from the discarnate helped us see the entity we were dealing with. They also made sure we were dealing with only one subject at a time, which relieved me of the concern that the contact would be broken into. These discarnate entities work with deep devotion to those in the earthbound realms, and where we might have worked only three or four nights a week, they work unceasingly to enlighten the forces of negative consciousness that pervade the earthbound plane.

Turning back to the incarnate members of the team, the channel was important to the research so that we could have a record of the responses from the discarnate side. In this work the channel is not a medium and generally has no psychic ability. A medium is most often associated with activities like a séance, and our activity was in no way a séance. It should be noted, though, that British researcher Lord Dowding—one of the most famous authorities on spiritual rescue work—during World War II, worked with a channel in trance, a rather well-known and respected medium who would go into a trance state, allowing the discarnate to speak through her. In our work, our channel remained fully passive but fully conscious and allowed herself to be used for automatic writing. Many people are sensitive enough to become channels. Automatic writing is an age-old form of astral-incarnate communication. A person sitting at a table with paper and pen in front of him is all that is needed. The channel relaxes his hand and allows the writing instrument to move in whatever direction and manner it chooses. Sometimes nothing but scribbles fill the page, and sometimes those scribbles begin to form letters, and later, words. In time, a well-practiced channel could start receiving a written message within a few minutes of sitting down.

When we worked, someone in the group would ask questions, and answers would come back from the discarnate earthbound individual in written form through the channel. What astounded us was how different the writing was in each case. The channel, who was not paying attention as the writing took place, was encouraged to look over the pages of notes at the end of the session and was often astonished by the different "hands" the writing encompassed. None of the writing styles were ever used by the channel in her own personal letter writing.

Some might wonder if the channel, or someone else, might have been interjecting their own thoughts into the material being transmitted. This might have some validity if it were not for the following: First, I had personally worked with this channel for better than three years and had observed her in minute detail in similar work. Second, the channel would have had to present an unending variety of vivid plots and life experiences on the spot, and they would have had to jibe with what I was seeing. And third, I tried, on a number of occasions, to induce information telepathically into the proceedings without success. I also asked the channel to try to influence the direction of the writing while it was taking place by trying to insert her own words or ideas. That also did not work. We had no influence over the messages that were written.

As we worked with each discarnate subject, the writing would often change considerably, in some cases from bold to light and from large to small, reflecting the emotional changes he or she was undergoing during the session. Emotional upheavals were captured on the page in spasmodic gyrations, and the released joy of the subject fairly manifested in bold script on the page.

The passivity of the channel did not, however, prevent some element of emotion from coming through and making itself felt. The intensity of the subject was often so great that the channel would suffer the same pangs of awakening and joy of release being felt by the earthbound individual. For this reason it was difficult, if not unwise, to attempt more than three or four cases in one sitting. However, the drain on the channel produced no ill effects that could not be easily extinguished by a short period of rest, relaxation, and a warm cup of tea following the sitting.

As the clairvoyant in this work, I fulfilled a much-needed position, that of being able to "see" what the subject's earthly background had been and therefore the major cause for his/her earthbound condition. Although this is a form of clairvoyance, in this work it went far beyond that. It could be said that I, too, was acting as a channel, only the information I received was from the discarnate workers and "X." These discarnate helpers and "X" did not work directly with the subjects. The subjects' state of consciousness and the fact that their attention was still caught up in the incarnate world made them unable to see and hear the discarnate workers. Any information we needed was strongly and vividly impressed upon my mind so I could ask the important questions that guided the direction of the session. To do this, I would literally have to "see" the subject so we could be kept aware of his actions and responses. Since clairvoyance was old hat to me, I was able to do this gladly and without discomfort. However, the clarity during this work was unlike anything else I've experienced.

And so the team was formed. The channel, the recorder, the researcher, and I on this side and "X" and his group on the other. Among us, we had the privilege of releasing many a soul from the confines of their self-made hell and assisting them in moving into the light of a compassionate world. Through a good stroke of intelligent fortune, we did not lose anyone in all of the people we worked with.

How We Worked

In our rescue work, we were concerned with that plane that was middle-lower class, and within this area, we focused our attention on those individuals who were willing and desirous of bettering their condition. However, because negativity is the dominant expression of earthbound individuals, we had to use extensive controls and regimentation. Without proper preparation and safeguards on our part, the members of the incarnate work group would have been at high risk for psychic harm if an earthbound subject, in order to satisfy his own desire, tried to possess someone vulnerable enough.

We seldom worked more than three nights a week and seldom did more than three cases a session. The decision to work this length of time was left completely up to us. Neither "X" nor anyone connected with him dictated any schedule or demands, nor did they deny us when we wanted to schedule a session. It was made evident that whenever we were ready to work, there would be more than enough subjects wanting our help. We did not choose a particular day of the week, preferring to work when both the channel and I felt physically and mentally competent. Physical or mental weariness of any kind was enough reason for us to cancel astral rescue work for the evening. We felt obligated to those we wished to help to present ourselves in the most capable posture possible because we had no way of knowing ahead of time what might be required of us or just how difficult the evening's work might be.

I have mentioned that we worked in the evening, but we also worked in the daytime. However, we did find daytime activity inconducive to focusing our full attention. Noise, interruptions, and the vibratory influence of the general activity in the neighborhood were distracting.

In preparing for a session, we set up a small table near a lamp and placed a notebook and a supply of pencils on the table. That was all the equipment we needed. But we found that other preparations were necessary on the mental-spiritual level. It was necessary for the channel to put herself in a state of complete passivity. At the same time, it was necessary for me to close my physical eyes and open my psychic eyes so I could see what was happening during the encounter. These states were accomplished by engaging in a period of complete relaxation, especially in the area of our mental faculties. When we were ready, I would contact "X" by simply sending a focused thought to him while maintaining a clear image of him in my mind.

We then went about establishing what I think of as the cylinder. The purpose of the cylinder was to ensure a level of security. Not only was this necessary to minimize influences, such as people passing by on the street and other common activity that usually invades one's home space, but also to ensure that we were in the best possible, non-invasive position while dealing with the negative conditions often emitted by our earthbound subjects. When dealing with negative discarnate entities, one must be aware that nothing vile or evil is beyond them. They would as willingly bring harm to the channel (since she was in a totally receptive state and could not protect herself) as they would to any entity they would confront in their discarnate surroundings. Earthbound entities are not usually cooperative and can focus their personal aggression on anyone. Again, they are living in a state of depression and pain, and their individual thought process flows toward those actions they think will give them the most power and relief. For this reason, a prerequisite in this work is the establishment of an area beyond their influence. This was accomplished when "X" took up his position directly above the channel and me. Now between "X" and us there flowed a powerful but unseen energy field strong enough to prevent penetration from negative entities on the discarnate side. This cylinder can be likened to a tunnel of light, with "X" at the top and us at the bottom. We referred to it as the cylinder of protection. To attempt astral contact in the manner and for the purpose we pursued, without considering the need for security and the possible consequences without such a format, invites lifelong spiritual and psychological damage to the channel and the other members of the group.

Having established the cylinder, we were in a position to invite the subject in; the entrance to the cylinder was controlled on the etheric side by "X" and the other discarnate helpers. The earthbound subject who pushed and bullied his way in was usually the first person we had to deal with. Sometimes the conditions around the cylinder entry were so chaotic that I had to call on "X" to sort things out. This was particularly necessary when two or more discarnates wanting immediate attention managed to jam themselves into the cylinder at once. It was up to "X" to sort them out. When that was accomplished, we could begin the session.

During an actual session, I would conduct an interview with the earthbound individual and ask questions to help bring him around to where he could be released from his negative state. I spoke out loud to the subject, and his reply was recorded by our channel through automatic writing. It was not really necessary for me to speak out loud, but the use of spoken conversation served two purposes: It was an effective way of holding the discarnate's concentration, and it allowed the session to be recorded so that those sitting in could hear the line of questioning.

We worked with more males than females. Not only are males generally more assertive, but they also tend to be more oriented to immortality. So when they didn't see their existence as a continuation of their life on earth, they were upset and wanted to know what the hell was going on. The females tended to be more timid and usually bided their time in the earthbound quietly. As Mary Ann T. explained when asked what she did there, "I just sit here and knit and sew and mind my own business."

Timing is all important. Moving too fast or too slow could send the whole session down the drain. The difficulty is that the timing involved has nothing to do with seconds or minutes. It is the kind of timing that a batter uses to meet the ball full out and put it past the outfield, or that of a boxer who, in a split instant, breaks through his opponent's guard and lands the telling blow that ends the match.

It did not take many sessions to discover that bringing our subject to a point of spiritual realization could be accomplished relatively quickly. By getting them to recognize what they had done to put themselves in that earthbound condition and getting them to understand what caused their present condition, we could usually move them to resolution without a long, drawn-out discussion. We also learned, however, that it was important to build a rapport with the subjects so that they could consider us friends who could be trusted. It became evident that, because of their negative consciousness, their span of concentration was quite limited. Unless we could maintain their interest and attention, they would leave the cylinder and return to their earthbound state.

The difficulty in concentrating led to the unfortunate problem of the earthbound discarnate not remembering his name, when he was born, or where he had lived when he was incarnate. On more than one occasion, we were given the name of someone who was well-known during his or her incarnation and would be easily recognized by name or position as being a public figure. Before we learned that the personal information the earthbound subjects gave us was suspect, we would go to the encyclopedia after the session to verify what we'd been told. To our dismay, we could not find one fact that checked out. Upset and a bit despondent, we appealed to "X" for an explanation. "X's" explanation added such an important dimension to our understanding of our undertaking that I will quote it directly:

> When a being leaves the earth plane, the physical senses are stilled to some degree, but upon arriving at this etheric level of rescue, there is a heightened awareness of identity and condition. But at the same time, almost all earth memory is blocked out, especially that of clock and calendar time. That remains so until such a time as a point of spiritual awareness is achieved. The rescue work is essential, but as you may surmise, the stories can be true or very far-fetched. That depends on the subject's degree of understanding as to what has happened to him and where he is at this time. How does one validate the information? That is not the issue. The only issue is that we are present and receptive, which gives them a desire to communicate and involve themselves in the rescue process. Many refuse when asked if they would like to find a way out of the depressing atmosphere or to communicate with us. We have no way to induce them to remember facts with any accuracy or even to give their true names. Would you cease

*to help them if they couldn't prove their earthly
identification?*

It was the last sentence of his communication that made
me feel ashamed. How often do we deny the plea of someone
in need simply because we have not been given enough
"facts"? There are times and events in life that call upon our
faith, not our intellect. We decided then, without hesitation,
that we should move ahead without that information.

Of course we were faced with the possibility that each
case was nothing more than a fantasy and that nothing
recounted by the contact was true. Although that might well
be, "X" reminded us that their story did not detract one iota
from the fact that these individuals were earthbound, that
they were miserable and in need of spiritual help, and that
the details of how they died and their earth life didn't matter.
Our only concerns should be where they were and how they
were feeling right then and their desire to become spiritually
aware. I must add, however, that there was enough
authenticity that we believed much of what the subjects told
us. As for those subjects who readily admitted that they
could not remember the year they died or other minor
matters that were part of their incarnate life, we stopped that
line of questioning and moved on to other areas of interest.

Our conversations with the subjects brought manifold
benefits. First, our conversations brought them to a point of
being more in touch with the reality of their situation. This
was vital; for up to that point, they had had no idea where
they were and what was going on around them. By
submitting to our questioning, the subjects were made to
think about their death experience and subsequent transition
to the earthbound plane. Those moments broke their sense of
being nowhere, and they became an identity able to evaluate
their place and condition. Another benefit derived from the
questioning was that, when the subject *could* remember and
was receptive, "X" could bring into the cylinder a discarnate

entity that the subject had had an association with during his incarnate lifetime. Sometimes it was a relative or a close friend, but it really didn't matter as long as the subject recognized the individual. This recognition always produced a dramatic shock to the subjects, because they knew that this was a person who had passed on. That immediate awareness broke through the sensation of being in a dream state, and the subjects became aware of their own position and where they were. Such confrontation in the earthbound has a tremendous impact and dispels the subject's belief that the event is only a transitory fantasy. This would then be reinforced by the discarnate helper's undeniably radiant state, the intensity of which exceeded anything the subject could experience in a dream. Quite often that awareness was enough to shock the subject into the reality of his condition and produce in him a basic desire to do whatever was necessary to orient himself to his new surroundings.

This shock of awareness caused another condition in the individual that proved helpful to us. When the subject was brought into our area of activity, he could see only one thing at a time, that which had, for whatever reason, caught his attention. In one sense this was a blessing, since we would have had a chaotic time dealing with a subject whose interest skipped like a thistle in the wind. One way to look at the problem they face is that it is like being lost in an unfamiliar place and having no idea how to get back to someplace familiar. It can be frightening in the incarnate world and downright terrifying on the earthbound plane.

The subjects, upon arriving in the cylinder of protection, did not see "X." They saw only the end of the cylinder where the channel and I were, mainly because they normally focused their attention on the incarnate world. Many wondered why they could no longer participate in events that had been common to their lifetime. As long as earthbound souls focus on the material world, they cannot elevate themselves to a higher plane. They simply cannot be two places at once, and the rule is, what you see is what you get.

In dealing with each subject, we carefully and patiently redirected his attention to "X." Although this doesn't sound like it would require great effort, it did, for every move was critical in getting this earthbound entity to release his hold on the earth life he once knew. Once we had the subject's attention, we would ask a series of questions aimed at getting him to identify "X." Once we accomplished that, we knew we had the subject's full attention, and the rescue work could proceed. This was not such a simple thing. These individuals were so fearful, confused, and caught up in their negative beliefs that they gave us answers that ran from outrageous to hysterical in an effort to mislead or distract us.

Ending a session properly was just as important as the format we used to begin the session. At the end of the interview, we couldn't just say thanks and leave. To simply dismiss the subjects after working so hard to get their attention would throw them back into their confusion. We developed a way to release the subjects from their focus on us and put them in a state where they could finally move onward. We had them perform a series of physical turns in response to military-type commands—make a quarter turn to the right, for example. I tried to get them to follow a command so that when they were finished they would be face-to-face with a discarnate worker, their astral escort, who would see to it that they were led away to continue their spiritual development. These face-to-face encounters were the emotional highlight of the session, not unlike the impact of a fireworks display—awesome, exciting, and radiant with joy. It proved a fitting conclusion, a graduation of sorts, before they journeyed forth into a new life.

When we were ready to end for the evening, we would tell "X" that we wished to conclude the contact, thank him for his invaluable assistance, and get up from the table. We then needed a cooling down period. It is hard to explain just how intense and charged up one becomes during these sessions, as well as being a bit disoriented after an evening of being so focused on the etheric plane and somewhat out of contact with our own earthly reality. We made tea and discussed the session, often feeling a great sense of accomplishment. Most of us enjoyed an exceptionally deep and restful sleep on the evenings we had worked.

Case Histories

The volume of material gathered during this work is too overwhelming to present here, so I have chosen to focus on a few case histories. There is much to be learned from them. The knowledge they offer is a legacy to those of us in the incarnate from those who have gone before and were willing to show us the pitfalls and wonders of the road ahead. It is impossible to express here the intensity of the anguish, hate, fear, doubt, joy, release, love, and rejuvenation expressed by the individuals who cooperated with us in this venture. To the doubter as well as the believer, the value of these case histories lies in keeping an open mind when evaluating the conditions they describe.

JOHN D.
The Revealer

We called John D. "The Revealer." John gave us valuable information about the earthbound. Most of the earthbound subjects we worked with lacked an understanding of their current state of consciousness and could not discern what was happening around them. We usually found them to be self-absorbed and reluctant to communicate. This was compounded by the fact that most of them had the attention span of a two-year old. John was different. Somehow he had broken through this self-absorption and was able to give us a better picture of what was going on in the earthbound, and for this, we were grateful.

John claimed he had been twenty-four years old when he passed on, and he was feeling cheated out of a normal lifetime. We found this attitude common among those who died before the age of thirty. Some subjects spent their time with us raging against their loss of life at such an early age. In John's case, as with others, he had wanted more out of life before he took advantage of the sweet side of heaven. Innately, we are committed to growth—physical, mental, and spiritual. Resisting growth is our attempt to hold back the ongoing energy of life, and we begin to suffer in some way or another. Death itself is a form of life growth. It allows the spirit to continue to grow through the experiences of natural transition. When that transition is resisted, there are consequences, for one cannot hold back the flow of life. John fought the transition, and the result was his arrival in the earthbound plane and an existence he abhorred.

John said he died in 1959. He had been divorced and claimed his wife "ran off with another guy." There were no children in the marriage. John insisted that his wife was infertile. He told us he was killed when he was hit by a streetcar in Chicago. He was then quick to point out that there were no more streetcars in Chicago, only the elevated, meaning the transit lines that run above the streets. (Remember, our subjects would give us any information they believed in, sometimes contradictory. After we discovered that much of their earth memory was faulty, we stopped devoting long hours toward researching their claims. Unless they would make an outrageous statement we knew to be untrue, we usually did not bother to question them on these points.) John claimed that he had been a steeplejack working on the elevated train system maintaining the higher tower supports. He made a point of assuring us that, "The money was good."

We turned our questioning to his funeral and immediately sensed his discomfort. We asked him if he had attended his funeral, and he said he had. (We found this was more common than we had imagined. Apparently many individuals attend their own funerals. As we urged John to give us more information, we began to feel that the funeral service and what is said there carries far more importance to the departed than may be imagined.) When we asked for more details, the writing became larger and more intense. Apparently this was a sensitive subject. John wrote, "I was just sick! Nobody but my working pals showed up!" The feeling of emotion and anger overwhelmed us. I was aware that our medium was deeply shaken. My impulse was to stop the proceedings right then, but breaking off contact so abruptly could cause a whole series of problems both for us and for the etheric side. I said nothing. There was a long pause. I thought we had lost contact with John, but I didn't want to say anything that might upset the delicate balance between us. We waited. Seconds ticked off, but I kept silent. The channel was composed but sad.

Just about at the point when I was going to go ahead and end the session, John began communicating again. "I don't want to be dead," appeared on the paper, with a long tail trailing from the end of the "d." The pencil moved, aimlessly wandering down the page and going up again. It changed direction and moved horizontally, making mounds and wave forms. I felt that as long as John was maintaining contact I would be patient and let him decide what the next move would be.

The pencil stopped. For seconds there was no movement. Then, in heavily impressed lines he wrote again, "I don't want to be dead. I want to go back and live my life out. I was having a better time there and not much at that, but this place is full of morons screaming and crying."

I asked him about the accident that killed him.

"Well, I didn't leave until about an hour or so [after he died], and I hurt like hell. Oh man, it still hurts, but not as much ... and I screamed and yelled and called for help and no one came. So I said, 'If there is a God, I've got two words for you!'" He admitted they were unprintable.

A person killed in some sort of violent situation does not necessarily immediately depart the location at which he died. The death transition can also include the sense that the body is still active and intact and therefore in pain, and that sense of pain can be carried by the consciousness to the discarnate plane with intensity.

He claimed that with all his yelling and calling for help, no one came. But I knew that that wasn't true. There is always someone on the other side to meet those who have passed over. I pressed John on this subject, and he finally admitted that there was someone who had come to him.

"I saw a woman or someone in robes and I told her to get lost," he said. I asked him if this person was trying to get him to go with her, and he admitted that she did, but he "didn't want to go where spooks are." Then he added emphatically, "I wanted to live again!"

Just as no human birth can take place without a female being present, no death, which is a form of birth, can occur without someone being present to assist. This may be a family member or a friend who passed on before us or simply a discarnate worker who, in devotion and love, has dedicated himself to this service. Such a worker was present when John made his transition. In his case, the worker had appeared as a female and someone he did not know. But he would not accept the offer of assistance. Refusing the help being offered by the worker played a major role in obstructing the ongoing journey of his passing spirit. John had made his refusal to accept help even more intense when he kept telling the discarnate worker to go away, that he didn't want any help, not from it or anything like it. We asked if he didn't get a good feeling from the discarnate worker, and he claimed that he had been "too shook up" to notice.

"John," I asked, "you talked about having a chance here. Who gave you this chance?"

"These men here with lights on said so," he answered.

"Do you see them now?" I asked.

"Yes."

"Tell me about them."

"They're all very tall and fair ... [long pause] wearing light robes that seem to be lit up inside and out. I've watched them for a while," he told us. "Weeks or so. And they come here and offer us this opportunity if we want it or not."

"What do they say to you?"

"'Sons and daughters, you see our light. You too may have light. Would you like to find out how?'"

"What do they say when you say yes?" I asked.

"Then they say, 'Those who desire light, form here, and you will be in contact with Earth and people there who are going to tell you how to make the change.'"

"Do many take advantage of this offer?"

"Sometimes a lot, like today. Sometimes not."

"Why don't they?"

"They don't believe them."

"Why did you believe them?"

"I figure what have I got to lose? I can't stand it here much more."

"What is it like there?"

"Like the movie *Snake Pit*."

John was ready to leave the earthbound. We took him through the military-like turns, then asked what he saw.

"I see another one, a man or lights. Even brighter than the workers outside the cylinder and in blue light," he said. Then he reported, "He smiled and feels warm."

"Who is it?" I asked.

"I don't know him," John answered.

"Are you sure it's a him?"

"Got a dress on," said John.

"Well, it's not a him," I said. "It's a she. Do you recognize her?"

"Sort of. [Long pause.] The lady who came during the accident."

The worker offered her hand to him, and he took it. He addressed us one more time before he left. "Thank you. Those fellows working for you up here really know what they're talking about. I'll tell the others when I leave to come see you. So long. And thanks again."

The Law of Free Will does not terminate with death. We have choice both now and in the hereafter. I can't help but feel that one of our great human defects is that we don't recognize this power and the potential it affords us. We can get what we want, whether it be good or ill. That is our great authority as spiritual beings.

MARY W.
Give Us This Day

We learned early in our work never to judge the importance of a case by its brevity. We found that many of the earthbound entities that came to us for help were so anxious to get out of their negative situation that they were as instrumental as we were in getting themselves on their way. Such was the case of Mary W.

It is hard for those who have not suffered hunger to imagine the power an empty stomach has on the consciousness. And, as is usually the case, the power is one of negation. It is a wise person who knows you can't talk about God to a hungry man. To Mary W., a God that allowed hunger was not worthy of any belief or faith, and in her anger over this, she carved out a place for herself in the earthbound.

Mary claimed to have been born in Sussex, England. When we asked the cause of her death, she replied, "A severe pneumonia and anemia ... hungry, that's what!"

A person's attitude about God, whomever they consider that to be, is primary to their state of consciousness. When we asked Mary about the conditions at her death, she was angry. "How could there be a God?" she complained. "I prayed when I was small for food and warmth for me and my family, and they is [sic] all dying of hunger!"

She brought another issue to our attention and that was how one can still maintain a strong emotional tie to those left behind. When we asked Mary if she had left a family behind when she passed over, her reply was, "They all cried, and I couldn't touch them or love them. Oh, my poor darlings!" So emotionally deep was that statement that two visitors to our group that night had tears in their eyes.

It is not uncommon in any part of the earthbound for discarnates of like condition to come together. Sometimes they form groups, sometimes mobs, and in some cases they knit themselves so intensely to one another that they form spiritual knots. Mary had such a group made up of Susan D. and Nancy C. By her own admission, Mary was "their protector." She insisted that we work with her charges, but we convinced her, after some discussion, that we could work with only one person at a time. She eventually conceded when we made it clear that we would see to Susan and Nancy at the first opportunity.

We were also a bit surprised at how astute Mary was, considering she'd had little education while incarnated. Her thoughts were clear, and she expressed herself in a manner that left no doubt in our minds what her issue was. We also saw that in some circumstances, life's difficulties can bring out great courage in a person, and it was evident that Mary had plenty of that to sustain her through those painful years of her earth life.

Fortunately, her desire for help was so strong that bringing her to the point of release was simple.

"Are you happy where you are?" I asked.

"No, I'm miserable," said Mary.

"What's to do?"

"Nothing, nothing."

I asked if she wanted our help.

"Yes," she said. There was a pause. "That's why I'm here."

I asked if she had seen other people leave that place that night.

"I had to ask you where they were going."

I told her they were being taken to a nice, clean, lovely place and asked if she wanted to go there. She said she would if her friends could go, too. Her friends, Susan and Nancy, were still on the sidelines watching.

"Do you remember your Uncle Oscar?" I asked.

"Yes. He was my mother's brother."

We did the military-type turns so she would see Oscar, who had been brought in by "X." Because it's so dark where they are, I asked what she could see. "Do you see a man standing there? Do you see any color with him?"

"Blue, beautiful blue," she said. "Is he an angel?"

"No, he's not an angel."

"Well I'm ready to be lifted up, and I'm ready to go with him. Why, it's ... it's Uncle Oscar!"

We watched as she was reunited with a loved one she thought she'd never see again. Clearly, the great courage that had sustained her in the incarnate was still in force in the earthbound, for when we began the process of release, Mary took over and was gone before we knew it as Oscar escorted her, Susan, and Nancy to the other side. She had been such a joy to deal with that we ended the evening's session after that, fully gratified to discover that a soul's courage doesn't diminish in the hereafter.

JACK C.
It's Cold as Hell

Jack, by his own admission, was a promoter, and he didn't worry too much about what he promoted as long as he could make a few bucks on the deal. He lacked any sense of moral or spiritual conscience and followed his greed wherever it took him. Although we knew he probably had many stories to tell, there was only one he wanted to talk about.

He had come in contact with an elderly woman when he was selling insurance. He was aware her finances were limited, but that didn't stop him from giving her the "full court press" and loading her up with insurance that she not only didn't need but couldn't afford. In order to make his commission, he badgered her into making payments at frequent intervals, something not required under the terms of the policy and technically illegal. He bled the woman financially dry. Without her small savings and with no family support, she became ill and died. Jack had made one of his friends the beneficiary of the policy, so they collected on the policy and pocketed the money. Under our questioning, Jack showed no remorse over this and stated that he didn't care "who it was that got took."

Some years after that incident, Jack became ill. He was rushed to the hospital, where it was discovered he had a perforated ulcer. Rushed to the operating room, Jack knew he was dying. As he put it, "I knew I was doomed!" That state of mind will send anyone to the earthbound. The death transition becomes intensely guilt-ridden and chaotic instead of calm and seamless.

Now in the earthbound, Jack knew where he was and felt he did not deserve anything better. Spiritual issues were out of the question, because Jack was convinced that God punished you and was intent on "getting even" with you if you had done the wrong things in your life. Jack gave into those beliefs completely.

But Jack's session opened up a new door for us. Up to this time, the description of the conditions our subjects found in the earthbound was pretty much the same. We never got much information because our discarnates, for the most part, didn't want to discuss their surroundings in detail. But when we questioned Jack about the earthbound, he was impatient to answer our questions. He made it clear that "hell" was not a place of fire and brimstone.

"Rough as cob," he said, "and twice as dirty ... no light ... cloudy ... rainy ... cold ... no fires even." He asked us, "Where is hell? No fires here. How does a guy get warm?" These impressions of the negative discarnate make sense when one considers that love is always thought of as a warm experience, and hate and loneliness are defined as isolating and cold. Jack's bit of "teaching" let us know that one does not burn for one's sins, but rather, one freezes for them and does so to the degree that the warmth of divine love is absent in one's consciousness.

Somehow, to me at least, the prospect of a barren, bone-chilling afterlife is much more foreboding than the thought of a fiery pit. In a later discussion of this, the team seemed to agree that it might be better if we were taught early on that sin is a heart-chilling experience that can be reversed by the warmth of love. After all, most of us have gone through the experience of being icy cold then entering a room with a warm, crackling fire, which we gladly approached to slowly and pleasantly turn from frigid to warm.

What we believe conditions will be after we break free of our physical bonds is exactly what we are going to find on the other side, and we knew from our many contacts over a long period of time that "hell" has numerous feelings and images. One experiences what the conscious mind believes to be true, and that self-recrimination plays itself out in a most negative scenario. If our life incarnate appears in bleak perspective, then our life in the hereafter will also be dark, cold, and foreboding. We each make our own heaven or hell every day of our life here on Earth. For Jack, as for all our discarnate subjects, the willingness to change, to let something new into their awareness, and the act of physically changing their perspective by performing the movements and turns we directed all helped to reorient their mental perception of themselves and of the possibilities awaiting them in the discarnate.

LLOYD C.
Desert of Despair

We often found that dealing with young men not yet out of their twenties who had passed into the earthbound was no mean task. The natural drive of youth, the feeling of being deprived of life, and a lack of spiritual awareness all combined to present a hard and embittered personality. Lloyd C. was an outstanding example of this.

Like John, Lloyd had been twenty-four when he passed over, and he protested, "just beginning life." Lloyd had been ill just before his death. He never told us what his illness was, but he was home at the time of his death. As he put it, "I felt I was going to die." When we asked him if he had sought help, he replied, "Why? I knew I was a goner."

This sense of imminent death and helplessness was common in our experience with the earthbound population. It was as if these individuals accepted whatever condition they were in as irreversible and that any effort to change the situation would be met with failure.

Lloyd resented his early death and his unfortunate position in the earthbound and, at first, seemed very willing to be helped. But his desire for help wavered between hopelessness at any chance of getting out of his "revolting" earthbound state and a deep belief that somehow he would be rescued from his plight. He had never attempted to get well during his illness, giving in to the body's acceptance of impotency. He felt physically defeated and "knew that death was imminent." He was so committed to this belief that he refused to muster any fight for life when he was given the chance. His case was a classic in hopelessness and defeatism. His sense of impotency was deeply felt by our group, as if a heavy cloud had descended upon us.

It was further aggravated by his replies to our questions. When we asked if he wanted us to help, he put us off with, "I don't want to do anything." And when we made it clear that his participation was absolutely necessary if he was to get out of his present state, he told us again, "I don't want to do anything." When we tried to get him to cooperate, his usual reply was, "What the hell do I have to do that for?" Nothing seemed to interest him, and nothing we promised seemed to please him. He had been taken away from a world he knew and found himself in a dark, dungeon-like place. He didn't know where he was, he knew no one, he might have tried a few things to get out that didn't work, and he had given up. He was trapped by his unwillingness to believe that life does not end with death and his unwillingness to accept his own space and take responsibility for himself.

Further conversation brought out the fact that he had received little love in this lifetime. There was no one he could count on and no one in his life who had made any attempt to reach out to him and give him comfort. He was emotionally isolated and had no hope of being "found." The thought of being rescued only brought a lethargic response and words of disbelief. It made it difficult for us because we had no way of touching an area of remembrance in him that might recall someone who had cared for him. When we told him that we could help him break free of his present condition, he told us that he "didn't believe we could swing it." When we suggested that he be strong and help us, he put us off by claiming that he was "a lover, not a fighter." Yet at that same time, he claimed he wanted to "get out of this rut," referring to his earthbound state.

We seemed to be at an impasse and called upon "X" for help. That help came in the form of a grade school teacher Lloyd had loved dearly and who had treated him with great kindness and patience. When she appeared, the atmosphere exploded with an emotion so intense it seemed to light up the whole room. Imagine being lost in the desert for years and at the point where all hope has been abandoned, you are found and rescued by the person who had meant the most to you in life. That was what was happening, and it was so deep and embracing, we were in awe.

MYRON P., MARVIN L., WILLIAM A. (& MONTE)
The Soldiers

We learned that chaotic conditions in the incarnate at the moment of death affect an individual's passage into the discarnate. In our experience, those in the earthbound who had died in battle experienced some of the greatest intensity and chaos when making their transition. When one moment you are alive, and in the next split-second, your life is severed by a bullet or shrapnel, there is little time for the consciousness to adjust to the change of condition, and the transition can be highly traumatic. This abruptness usually causes those involved in battle to enter the discarnate through the earthbound, unaware they have passed on.

Here are the cases of three soldiers we worked with who had been killed in battle. The first died around 1100 A.D., the second during the U.S. Civil War, and the third during World War I.

Myron P. claimed that he was killed in 1102 in Spain. We had reason to doubt this because we'd had trouble with him and his responses from the beginning. He gave us his last name spelled two different ways. When we questioned him about his first name and nationality, he begged indifference.

He didn't claim to need help but readily admitted that he was still engaged in wartime activities. His answers were generally evasive but not defensive. He claimed he was a military scout, but when pressed for details, he avoided questions by saying, "I am doing my job."

His turnaround was quick. He was quite willing to talk to "X." He rapidly grasped and accepted what was being offered to him. I attributed that to his consciousness being ready to release itself from battle. When we reached the point where he could be released to the discarnate crew, he left with an air of indifference, giving us the feeling that his military experience didn't leave him with much trust. Nevertheless, the transition was made, and that pleased us.

Our second soldier was Marvin L. His case was one we remember for the joyful emotion that spilled over from his consciousness during his awakening. Marvin could not remember in what year he had died, but in a rather left-handed fashion he indicated that it was during the U.S. Civil War. He claimed that he'd died at home from wounds received in battle but made it clear he was not killed in action.

Before the war came along, Marvin had been a young, happy-go-lucky boy. He had no spiritual awareness and had given no thought to death or possible afterlife experiences. (We found that a large dose of spiritual ignorance during one's incarnate state can have a major effect in the life hereafter.) In Marvin's case, death came so quickly and unexpectedly that he was completely disoriented. When we met him, he was in deep depression. He talked angrily about the "dirty, rotten animals" that surrounded him in the earthbound. He was excited about leaving that area, and we had some trouble containing his excitement so we could finish the procedure. This was manifesting in his writing, which became so exuberant that we could hardly make out the words. But we got him under control and finished the process. His last words were, "I got a small parcel of land, and I give it to you for all your help." Of course, he had no land where he was, but it was a generous gesture.

William A. was another young soldier who was unaware that he'd been killed. His initial attitude in dealing with us was one of devil-may-care, give 'em hell, which was typical of many of the young men who went into battle in World War I.

When I asked for his name, he answered, "Roger Dodger," an old army phrase used during World War I.

I censured him a bit. "I'm not going to have anything to do with you if you don't behave yourself."

"Says who? Catch me if you can."

William was so flippant and aggressive that rather than risk harm to the channel by some means I might not be aware of, I stopped the interview in order to check with "X" and get some additional background on William. The information was quickly provided and put me in a position of exercising greater control over the situation.

I noticed someone was with him and asked him who it was.

"That's Monte."

"Are you having a good time?" I asked.

"Rip roaring," he answered.

I asked him if the war was still on.

"Yup."

William and Monte had been killed at the same time, and neither realized that they were dead and in the earthbound. As far as they were concerned, they were still on earth, fighting.

"Don't you get tired of fighting?"

"Sometimes."

"Do you know that you're dead?"

"No! You're kidding!"

"No, I'm not. You've passed on."

"Well then, where am I?"

I told him he was in the earthbound condition.

"I'm a rotter." (An English phrase meaning not a good person, kind of a bum.) I asked if he wanted help, and he asked if things would be better.

"Yes," I said. "There wouldn't be any more fighting. You'd feel good."

His reply was a huge, "Yes!" with fourteen exclamation marks.

I asked if Monte would like to be helped too. There was a very long pause while he went to check it out. "He says it's okay," said William.

Then we started the body movement work with both of them to get their focus. When I was talking to William, he recognized someone who waiting for them.

"Tell me what he looks like," I said.

"Young ... blond ... it hurts ... the light ... my eyes," he said.

After the dark earthbound state, the light can be blinding at first. The earthbound subjects are almost always impressed that the worker is brightly colored—usually white, blue, or blue-white. Frequently, it is also someone they knew in life.

"Do you remember the battle you were killed in?" I asked.

"Oh my god! ... It's Cap!" he shouted, recognizing the captain that he and Monte had served under and who had been killed earlier in the war. The former commanding officer took both of them.

Although the trauma associated with a killed-in-action scenario is painful, there is also hope that all will turn out right. I think it comes from a soldier's belief that he is going to make it, and even when he doesn't, his faith keeps him believing that, in the end, all will turn out right and he will be saved.

POLLY K.
Perpetuating Pain

What is the source of pain? When the body is in pain, is the mind in pain also? How much pain can one overcome? Is dealing with physical pain strictly mind over matter? In the case of Polly K., we were significantly impressed that mind and matter are inseparable.

Polly had lived a life of pain, both mental and physical. A cripple raised in an orphanage, she knew neither health nor love. Like many, she raged at God for giving her these awful handicaps. Pain was her constant companion. Then, as if it needed to stage a grand finale, it burst forth in all its fury when, on her way home at three thirty in the morning from her job as a cleaning woman in an office building, the bus she was riding in blew up, killing her. She claimed that she was the only passenger and that the driver was also killed in the explosion.

Death had not released her from pain's grip. Her consciousness, so pain-filled on earth, continued to produce its domination of her senses in the discarnate state. So vivid was her consciousness that she could pinpoint the exact areas of her "body" that bothered her most. It was interesting to compare her condition to that of others who had suffered grievous bodily harm. The soldiers, for instance. They, too, had suffered significant bodily harm, but the pain associated with that had not prevailed in their consciousness after their transition. With Polly, however, pain had been such a conscious focus of her existence on earth that her passing only magnified the condition.

With "X" assisting, the "terrible pain in her leg" was eradicated. As small a gesture as that was, it was enough to turn her consciousness away from dwelling on this lifelong pain to the freedom of once again being whole.

This case helped focus on the question of belief. In Polly's case, the belief that she would never have relief from pain kept her in a state of suffering. It begs the question: Can one relieve suffering by consciously focusing on a condition completely removed from that of physical pain? If this refocusing is done with strong intent, would the existing pain recede and perhaps disappear altogether? Many have proven that this method can be successful with strong convictions and a cooperative, focused mind working in tandem with professional medical help. Polly's lifelong experience with pain is not a condition that others have to endure.

JOHN & BETTY M.
Money Is the Root

This case is interesting because it carries with it undertones still familiar in this day and age—the business of working hard so that one might have money to buy things and then working harder to keep them and to buy more. Credit buying was not common during John's lifetime, which he claimed was around 1936. Still, the results of striving hard for material goods brought the same financial and psychological issues that would have come about had he been heavily burdened with credit card debt.

John was married to Betty, a woman who wanted "things." His story, which we didn't doubt, was that he was just one big paycheck to his wife. He worked hard, and she spent hard; then, he worked harder. In all things, good or bad, there seems to be a limit, a time when something inside us shouts a command to halt. To someone with strong discipline, that often means nothing more than retrenching and regrouping one's forces so that the situation can be brought back into balance. To someone without a spiritual foundation of support, stopping is only a momentary respite in which the pendulum wavers at the top of its arc before plunging downward on its inexorable swing to the other extreme. Such was the case with John.

Betty's unreasonable demand for material things began to grind out a pattern. He said he was not happy.

"I felt I had to earn that paycheck to pay for ... for THINGS!"

"What kind of things?" I asked.

"You know, above the normal things you need." He said the harder he worked, the more Betty spent. I asked if he started drinking before his death.

"A little or I would have lost my mind."

"I don't think it was a little," I told him. "I think it was quite a bit."

"I guess it was."

He said the extra money on his job was "for ME!" I asked how he got the extra money.

"Well, you're smart, you seem to know."

"Yes, I do know, but I want you to tell me anyhow."

"I rigged the books."

"How much did you take?"

"Just a few thousand." Then he added, "My wife caused the whole thing. She drove me to take the money."

The prospect of an upcoming audit of his books triggered his passing by way of a massive heart attack. What had begun as simple resentment had evolved into hate and, with it, a strong desire to get some extra money for things that *he* wanted. As his deficit at work grew, so did his hate for his wife and the world around him. Even his spiritual values suffered as he went from belief to a rage focused on a higher power to which he assigned considerable blame for his plight. The amount of hate he had built up within himself assured him entry to the earthbound level of the discarnate.

There are other points of interest with this story. John was very much aware that his anger against Betty and the negative feelings he fostered toward his relationship with her were spiritually dangerous. He alluded to this fact when he told us, "It's bad for me now because I'm still hating her." In those few words, he let us know he was aware of the negative force he had created and that he was the primary source of his unfortunate condition in the astral state. Those in the earthbound seldom recognize how they create their own agony, so we were taken aback by his insight.

"Would you like to get out of there?" I asked.

"Yes," he said, "I feel I'm not getting any place. What's the use in hating her? Can't help things now."

As it so happened, John's wife was in the earthbound as well. She was there because she was convinced he had died "just to make things tough on me!" She was just as angry and resentful as he. By this time, "X" had brought Betty into the cylinder.

John saw the helper first, blue with a white outline. Then I had him turn 180 degrees.

"It looks like Mr. B.," he said.

"No."

"I can't tell," he said.

"You must tell me, John." Long, long pause. Then, in tiny, tiny writing, he said, "My wife."

"Yes," I said, "and you're both being held by the hate you have. Now you can be free."

He said, "We will go together."

"Not yet," I said. There needed to be some bonding first, and they needed to release each other before they could move on. Unless each forgave the other, neither was going to advance.

"God forgive me," John said, "and release this bondage."

He told me, "She has come and embraced me. [Pause.] With love."

They were paired together again, and the embrace radiated with love.

Their joint recognition gave us a unique opportunity to work with a couple who had been married in their earth life and the privilege of bringing about their release together.

When they had recognized their position and realized that under all that hate there was still a foundation of love and affection, they became a powerful spiritual unity. It made us realize how much could be accomplished when true love is set free. As the master teacher said, "Love can move mountains." In the case of John and Betty, it not only moved their mountains of hate, but it opened up a vista of eternal love and light.

REBA G.
Angels of Color

It would be wonderful if we could be just one, big, happy household of humanity. But the reality is that our household has many, many walls constructed of misshapen beliefs and prejudices, some of which were built with legitimate justification. Yet regardless of how justified their construction, the walls must be scaled.

I was a little surprised when Reba G. arrived because she was the first African-American discarnate we had worked with. And her awareness of my surprise almost caused us to lose the opportunity to work with her, since she interpreted my reaction as one of disapproval.

Reba had spent her lifetime suffering under the authority of white masters. This, and having witnessed cruelty and abuse toward her daughter, had made Reba wary and hateful toward anyone who did not share her dark skin. This deep hatred brought her to the earthbound.

"I'll never get along with you," she said.

"Why not?" I asked.

"'Cause you're white, and you'll never help a black person."

"How do you figure that?"

"Whites never did me any good."

Reba had worked on a plantation in the South. She had practically no religious belief because, as she put it, "God ain't gonna help no colored slave."

Reba had a daughter named Lindy. One summer day two young boys, sons of the plantation owner, found Reba and her daughter alone in the fields. The boys dismounted their horses and proceeded to tease and then rape the young girl. When Reba attempted to save her daughter, one of the boys remounted his horse and drove the horse into her, literally stomping her to death. No effort was made by authorities or the plantation owner to discover who had done this terrible deed. It went unpunished and was quickly forgotten. Reba's daughter was left in the field and eventually found her way back to the slave quarters. Nine months later, she died in childbirth.

The events of Reba's life quickly set up an almost immovable barrier toward anyone of white skin, including those of us in the incarnate group of the astral rescue team. If it were not for the misery of the earthbound plane, we probably would not have had any chance of helping her.

But even with her pain of being earthbound, it was obvious that we were going to need considerable help from the discarnate workers if we were to help her move on. Just the problem of the color line alone was a formidable obstacle. We had no option but to appeal to "X."

The assistance that came surprised us, for instead of bringing in the discarnate workers we usually worked with, "X" brought in a host of angels with dark skins. This was something we'd never seen before, as the positive discarnates have no skin color, as such. Reba almost exploded with delight and excitement when she saw these helpers from, as she called it, "the Calvary Mission." Her response was a heart-pounding series of, "Oh my goodness! Oh my goodness!" Reba's hate, fear, and bitterness began to dissolve as she stood in wonderment looking at the dark-skinned angels, afraid that if she moved they might disappear. We gave her time, and when we thought she had accepted them as reality, we urged her to go with them.

All her conscious resistance vanished, and the smile on her face was absolutely serene. Then everyone in the room heard it, music the likes of which we'd never experienced before — the refrain of the angels.

TONY C.
Mr. Tough

Tony C. was our full-fledged gangster. Joining a gang in his early teens and growing up to run dope for a syndicate, he knew only a life of crime on the streets. From our first moments with him, we saw a tough, hard-as-nails attitude spoiling for a fight. Pegged for assassination by a rival gang, he was shot in the back by a drive-by gunman. That event did not seem to make any difference in his attitude. When we first dealt with him, he made it clear that he was ready to lick the world.

But the earthbound condition is a great leveler, and as tough as he was, he could not cope with his life there. He wanted out. I'll always remember Tony's remark when we asked how it was in the earthbound. "Dead," he replied. "Lousy," he added.

Human denial, if allowed to grow, produces a hard shell around the consciousness. A person can make a prisoner of himself by cutting himself off from the world and from those who may be reaching out to him. Some of us need to be brought to our knees before we will release ourselves from our self-made mental prison and walk into the space of all-encompassing love. It can be done in life, or if necessary, after we die. That's where it happened for Tony.

Initially, we could not find someone who meant enough to him in his life and upon whom we could focus his consciousness. He detested his parents and everyone else who had been close to him, with one exception—Sally. Tony knew love only once in his life and that was when he was twelve years old. Even then, any surge of love was beaten back as if it were an enemy trying to scale the walls of the fortress. His awakening would be contingent upon our ability to break through his wall of resistance, not just by cracking it, but by shattering it into irreplaceable pieces.

What a struggle we had. Feeling rejected by the world and isolated at home, he felt Sally was unattainable. He worshipped her as only a young boy could worship a beautiful, young girl. To him, she was all the good in the world contained in one lovely being, and in his consciousness, he was convinced that he was not even worthy enough to touch the hem of her skirt.

When consciousness desires to reject a person or condition for whatever reason, it can, in fact, go blind. Tony would not accept help from anyone, much less from someone he felt was so far above him. The walls he had built around himself kept him from acknowledging Sally even when he knew that it was she who had come to help him. He fought us, argued, cursed, and raved. When we tried to recount the scene in which he had first met her, he became angry and yelled, "Don't bring all that back!" He took exceptionally long pauses before he would answer our questions. He insisted Sally was "not for me." He was a man having a private fight with the devil.

Fortunately in the end, the good guy won. Tony didn't try to send her away or deny her presence, and when he finally let himself recognize her, it was as sweet a reunion as any two lovers ever had. Some believe that love conquers all. In Tony's case, it was true in every sense of its passion.

JOHN M.R.O.
The Great Ego

I remember this case vividly because I had to work so hard to keep from laughing that I actually hurt from the effort. John's approach to his life's condition and subsequent departure was an experience with the human ego that was both astounding and farcical.

When incarnate, John was the image of the big, strong, invincible male who would, and could, meet any of life's challenges. He reveled in his strength and faced life with all the aplomb of superman on a mission to liberate the world from the evils of mankind. When we made the initial contact, the intensity of his ego and self-aggrandizement hit us like an unexpected storm raging its way across the open plains. It took us a few moments to catch our breath and regain our composure.

Good looking, dashing, a ladies' man without peer in his own hometown, John did nothing that was not dramatic and designed for effect. We had no idea how this bold and charming person would receive our interrogation, but it took only a few questions for us to find out that we had grabbed an alligator by the tail. Clearly, he was not going to say anything that could in any way diminish the image of the strong, heroic male. He made it clear to us that the way a man should leave this mortal world is by being shot in a great duel over a lady's honor or to lose his life by fighting a band of thieves intent on robbing his stagecoach carrying the governor's wife and beautiful daughter or in some other manner and action worthy of a statue in the town park hailing him for his chivalrous exploits. Such was his personal vision, and he swaggered his way through life as the Zorro who would retreat from no one. He had imagined his death would be nothing less than a magnificent act of gallantry. But fate had another scenario in mind, one that John was most reluctant to recount.

When we reached the point in our questioning where we wanted some information about how he had died, there was a long pause. The pencil stopped and then made little scratch marks, the kind of thing someone might make in the dirt with the toe of his boot when embarrassed. When we pressed the issue of his death, he answered with the complaint, "Who cares? I'm dead. Ain't that what you need—dead people?" I assured him that we did not "need" dead people, but that our purpose was to assist those who had died in understanding their current status. I asked him again about the cause of his death.

"Fever," he said.

"What kind of fever?"

"Syphilis," he said.

When I told him we did not believe that, he got defensive. "But I had it, though."

I allowed that he might have had syphilis at one time or another, but it wasn't the cause of his death. I asked again.

"Spinal meningitis."

I knew that this had not been the cause, because even after the spirit passes to the other side there remains some residual of any illness that had been particularly intrusive or damaging to the body incarnate, and there was none of that with John. So I asked again.

"Rat fever," he replied.

"No," I said, "that was not the cause."

"Diphtheria," he answered.

I began to wonder if we were going to have to sit through the whole physicians' manual of common diseases.

"T.B.," John said. "My lungs gave out."

We dismissed that answer. The writing then became very small, almost unintelligible. We had to squint to read it.

"Flu."

Before we could make a comment, he started writing again. The words were large and the sentences aggressive.

"Did you ever hear of such a damn thing?!" he complained. "I'm as husky as you, better than you. What the hell, a man keeps himself strong, and pow! One fell swoop, and it couldn't be a tumor or some horrible thing. Goddamn cold IN THE CHEST!!"

Well, we had to admit that dying of the flu was not nearly as adventuresome as scaling the walls of an enemy stronghold and fighting one's way through to the ammunition pile only to be shot as the last ammo keg was thrown over the wall. A bout with the flu was one Hollywood sequence that would have never made it off the cutting room floor, and John's great last moment was nothing more than a painful, hacking cough. It was too much for him to bear, and death had not lessened his embarrassment.

When our reality does not match our vision, we are disappointed, but usually we pick ourselves up and get on with life. But for John there was no getting on, except out of the earthbound, and for him to do that, he would have to give up his visions of grandeur that had failed to manifest. Death, John discovered, is the common denominator. You end up as you truly are, not as you wished yourself to be. As soon as he could accept that, he would be free.

He scratched his face and shuffled his feet. His disappointment was palpable. He wanted some way of escaping the truth, some way in which he would be the hero in a grand exit. We waited. He scratched some more. We waited.

Finally there was a sigh, followed by a cough. "Okay," he said, and he turned around to face the discarnate worker who had come for him. He acted like he was trying to cough again, but no sound came out. He was well. The "hero" had died in the end, but the spirit moved onward. As he straightened his shoulders, lifted his head, and walked away, we saw that this was a finale with far more impact than he had imagined.

MARY ANN T.
The Man Hater

In our world, differences and dislikes can quickly become extremes. This was evident to us in our session with Mary Ann.

Mary Ann claimed she was killed in a freak accident when she fell off the railing of her front porch and broke her neck. She didn't want to talk about the accident, so we moved on and asked if she'd been married. Her answer was a vehement, "NO!" written on the paper. She thought men were "dirty."

"About what?" I asked.

"Any- and everything," she replied. "They smoke, drink, carouse."

"Was your father like that?"

"Yes!"

"Did this make your mother unhappy?"

"Yes."

"Were you afraid of your father?"

"Sometimes."

I was trying to be as much a non-male entity as I could when talking to her. Also, because of where I was (incarnate) and where she was (discarnate) and the fact that we were in the cylinder of protection, she felt herself to be in neutral territory, and I was not looked upon as being aggressive or interrogating.

With further questioning, she admitted that her mother had lectured her many times on the "disgusting way men were." This home environment was the foundation of Mary Ann's education about male-female relationships. We allowed that other young girls had also faced difficult conditions at home with their fathers, but they had moved on and put it behind them. That approach got us nowhere. In fact, it opened the floodgates of her anger wider.

When I asked what religion she was, she drew small circles on the page and answered, "Nothing in particular."

"Does that question embarrass you?"

"Yes."

"Why does it embarrass you?"

"Because ministers are men too."

"Is that why you didn't go to church?"

"Yes."

"Didn't you ever pray to God?"

God was a male, she said, and she wouldn't allow herself to pray or have any other form of communication with him because, "He doesn't like women either."

Her conception of men was so off balance that she maintained a completely distorted view of even the simplest spiritual values if males were involved. Her anti-male attitude also included the Bible and accounts of the disciples. Her attitude and distortion were strong enough to put her in the earthbound.

I asked what kind of work she had done. She told me that she'd been a grade school teacher and that she'd liked it.

"What do you do now?" I asked.

"I just sit here and knit and sew and mind my own business."

"That's all? Are you happy doing that?"

"No," she said, "but I've learned to accept whatever may come."

"Don't you have any friends there?" I asked.

"No, I don't need any."

"Aren't there people around you?"

"Yes, but I ignore them," she said.

"Do they ignore you too?"

"Yes."

Then she told me that she felt like she was stuck in the mud.

"Mary Ann," I asked, "did you see those other people leave?"

"Yes."

"How did they look?"

"They have lights all over."

"Did they look happy?"

"Yes."

Her release from the earthbound would have to be made with the help of a male and her acceptance of him, otherwise there would be no change in her attitude and no onward development of her spirit. Again, "X" provided the help and a young man showed up who looked very much like the images we see in pictures depicting Jesus.

His presence was like a visual and mental explosion to Mary Ann, and she whirled around, putting her back to him and shutting her eyes. She wouldn't budge and refused to respond to our questions. Earlier in the session, she made it clear that no man could be loving and kind, and she was resolute now in her rejection of this male helper. We tried to get her attention, but she remained immobile.

Then the male rescue worker moved closer to her, radiating warmth and compassion toward her. She began to tremble but still refused to turn toward him. I tried talking to her, but she would not communicate with me. About the time I thought we should cut off contact, the man reached out and lightly touched her shoulder. I held my breath. The atmosphere around the table turned blue. It felt as if there was enough electricity in the air to power the lights of a city.

Mary Ann moved slightly, appearing at first as if she were going to walk away, but instead she slowly turned. All the loving light this etheric helper showed in his face now became reflected in her face. She stared at him for what seemed like minutes. Slowly, her body relaxed. The man stood still. She continued to stare at him for a long time, and then as if she had completely surrendered, she took his hand.

Her writing became small, almost childlike, "He ... he ... he is so beautiful," she wrote. The writing stopped, and she stood transfixed. This was a whole new world for her, a discovery and acceptance the magnitude of which she could not have imagined just a few moments earlier. Before we could ask another question, she wrote, "The whole sky has opened up, and sunshine is pouring through!" There was nothing else for us to ask.

Conclusion

What happens to the earthbounds after they are taken away by the astral helpers? Some go to the discarnate hospital to restore their spiritual energy. Some go to a transition area where they are offered help to come into full realization of their condition until they desire to go forward from there. They are offered learning sessions to explain the issues that put them into the earthbound and what they can now do to advance their life experience in the discarnate. This process leads to a whole new world of excitement and pleasure as they rediscover their true self. Once in the positive levels, they can recognize immediately this great expanse they're in and that they are more than they ever believed themselves to be. The wonderful thing about dying is the recognition of how expansive we are, lateral expansiveness, horizon after horizon. It makes you giddy.

I cannot say enough about the magnitude of assistance, love, and compassion offered, with the greatest devotion, by the astral workers. As earthbound souls grapple in the darkness they create, these working angels are always present, trying to engage them and show them the way out. In fact, the magnitude of assistance provided from the positive discarnate planes of the Earth School to both incarnate and discarnate individuals is phenomenal. Not just one guide or one-to-one help, but hundreds of millions of committed entities in the positive astral planes are assisting in the development of individuals in this difficult, post-graduate school.

While incarnate, each of us is assigned a band of five or more guides. They will not make choices for you or help you carry out your plans. They will not even advise you on choices. Their task is to inspire you, to hold up for you a mirror of truth so you can see your reflection as you make your choices. Whether or not you look into that mirror and let yourself see what is there is entirely up to you. They will not interfere with your free will.

Hand in hand with free will is karma, the Law of Cause and Effect. Karma means we can reap only what we have sown, regardless of whether it was done in a state of informed awareness or in a state of ignorance. We get back exactly what we put out. No exceptions. Bad thought will bring you bad people. Good thought will bring you good people. Bad thoughts will bring you bad life experiences. Good thoughts will bring you good life experiences. No one can weasel out of karma because it is the Law of the Universe. If karma were not in place, the Universe would be chaos.

The freedom we seek in life is still available to everyone in death. Failure to exercise that ability, however, compounds the darkness in the earthbound plane. We have frightfully many ways to express fear and ignorance: carelessness, greed, bitterness, despair, confusion, pain, blame, anger, self-isolation, folly, hatred. The negative planes are outpourings of the incessant negative thinking of the inhabitants. Yet we can take comfort in knowing that help is always available to us, and if we but choose, a small nudge can put us back on course to expanding our wisdom and our joy. It takes believing in ourselves and being willing to risk, for without first loosening its lines and sailing out to sea, no vessel can make it to another port. Let your faith and courage carry you beyond the horizon, and your soul will see you safely home.

Dying Well, Dying Consciously

You got to be careful if you don't know where you're going, because you might not get there.

— Yogi Berra

The only time death felt alarming to me after that was during combat. I spent thirteen years in the army, including eighteen months in combat in Korea. There, I saw people being violently yanked out of life as they understood it, and I knew that this shock and trauma was not how death was meant to be.

If we have to die, we may as well do it well, right? Most of us would choose to die by slipping away peacefully and quietly in the night. It would be like taking a walk in the woods on a deliciously sweet, early summer day and crossing over a river. On the other side, there would be one of our very favorite people, someone whom we haven't seen in ages, waiting for us with a welcoming smile. Can we help make our death such a pleasant experience? I believe we can. First, though, we must face our greatest fear. I said in the introduction that our greatest fear is death. I'd like to restate that now and say that, although we are afraid to die, most of us fear living even more.

Take the poor soul who goes off every morning in bumper-to-bumper traffic to a job he hates then returns home in more bumper-to-bumper traffic to eat dinner, watch TV, be with children he can't control, and go to bed with a woman he doesn't care for. What does his life say about him? While he may not actually say that he wishes he were dead, that is how he lives. It's a pretty good bet that he's afraid of death, too, so he doesn't think about it consciously. But his attitude and demeanor scream it and his body is listening. What he should be thinking about is living, but he's afraid of that, too. Instead, he numbs himself so that he will not have to confront tough questions looking for answers and challenges waiting to be met in the life lesson he has chosen.

How often do you wake up in the morning exhausted and dreading what's in front of you? We're surrounded by people who don't want to meet life on the terms they have set up. Are you one of those who lives in wait, believing that something outside of your control must change before you can make your life your own? Some feel trapped by circumstances. Some are angry because they aren't living in the surroundings they desire. Some think they don't have what it takes to fulfill their dreams. So they go through the motions of a day, using alcohol, drugs, food, television, noise, and "busy-ness" to avoid the real issues of their life.

Then there are the "because of" people, those who believe their purpose for living is because of others: because my children need me, because I'm taking care of Mother, because I'm the sole support of the family, because I'm indispensable to the smooth running of my company, community, church, or country, and the list goes on. In such thinking, their personal quality of life is not given consideration, only their degree of service. While there are those for whom service is their path, there are many who give themselves in service to others as a way of ignoring a strong pull to do something different, and chances are, personally more difficult.

Not only do we have myriad ways to numb our living, but we plan for death. We prepare for our absence by taking out life insurance, writing a will, setting up trust funds, and choosing how we'll be buried. While making plans for our family's financial well-being when we're gone is the right thing to do, when was the last time you approached living with such clarity of purpose and planning?

It is also true that most of us, at some time or another in our lives, spawn a conscious death wish. How often have you heard someone say he wished he were dead? I can think of these examples:

- The person whose life is depressing and unfulfilled.

- The person who feels so neglected that he starts a conversation about death and looks for a response from others to agree with his view of dying. This serves as a support to him and is the ultimate form of negative sympathy.

- The person whose anger has so engulfed him that he plans his demise to make people regret that they did not treat him well when he was alive. It's a form of, "I'll get even with you, then you'll be sorry you treated me this way."

- The person who would rather be a dead hero than a live nobody.

- The person who no longer seeks to believe in or pursue his creative ability.

- The person who, by character, is a risk-taker and is trying to prove that he can spit in the eye of life and get away with it.

- The person who feels that his life is going downhill, and rather than let that occur naturally, he makes a move to end his life in a more "regrettable way."

- The misguided individual who is convinced that he is worth more dead than alive because of his insurance — another form of misguided heroism.

- The person who has violated the law and cannot face public disgrace. He constantly thinks of dying, until he eventually has a heart attack or contracts a terminal disease.

- The person, usually elderly, who finds himself no longer able to live a healthy life or to do the things he would like to do and is tormented at the thought of being a burden to his family. Not only is it depressing, but it's scary as hell, and he wants out.

- The elderly person who has been there and done that for so long that he is truly tired of living. Although not consciously, such an individual would likely be in a space of death preparation.

We all can think of many reasons for wanting out of this incarnate experience. If you have had a conscious death wish, what do you think has prompted it? Depression? Loneliness? Hopelessness? Shame? Desperation? Fear of facing your future? Do you think life is a limiting, imprisoning, unpleasant experience and consistently find yourself thinking that your only release will be death? If so, something is amiss in how you're managing your life. Carrying such an attitude can submerge your consciousness below the level required for good health and put you in a space of unconscious death preparation. If your body is picking up on the feeling that you don't want to live, it's going to respond. You will become ill, or more ill as the case may be, and you will die—whether it takes days, weeks, months, or years—without having completed the learning you intended. How you are living right now is determining how you will die. If you are reluctant in accepting your natural freedom in the incarnate, it will obstruct your understanding of the options available to you during the death experience.

Toss out the idea that you're not supposed to be here and that your real life will begin when you die. You *are* supposed to be here, and it's a wonderful place to be. If you don't think so, you have some work to do. As dutifully as saying morning and evening prayers, you should stop and evaluate how you're handling your life. As part of that daily self-evaluation, rather than asking if you're a good person, ask if you are a *living* person. Do you feel alive? Do you feel excited and committed? Or are you ignoring this breathtaking opportunity? It's not about being able to do everything you'd like to do. It's about whether you are taking advantage of the opportunities available to you each day, or if, instead, you are giving your life away. As long as you breathe,[5] there is opportunity waiting for you. Don't die with regret. Die with the peace of knowing that you took full advantage of being here and embraced life completely. Leave knowledge, love, and good remembrances for those left behind. Nobody can live your life the way you can, and the performance of it is a singular gift.

One of our biggest fears is that we will suffer a drawn-out terminal illness that will cause us tremendous pain and make us a burden on the family. There are those who believe that people who are terminally ill and in great pain have the right to take their own lives. Again, suicide is the ultimate transgression against the Universe. None of us has the right to take a life, even our own. To consider using suicide as a way to control how your death will be is an ignorant and unfortunate choice. Your entrance to the other side will be weighted by this violation of Universal Law, and I can guarantee that this will not make your transition any easier. Physician-assisted suicide is also a transgression. It is a taking of life before its time, and even though it is done at one's

---

[5] From this, I exclude someone in a coma breathing only with the help of a machine.

request, the death is not really an act of total will on the part
of the individual. To bring about the death, it requires a drug
and outside parties to play a role. It is one thing to dictate a
codicil to your will that stipulates if you are on life support,
you want the life support to be pulled off. If you cannot
maintain life on your own, that is not suicide. If, however,
you take a pill to kill yourself, even if the body only has
months or weeks to live, it is suicide. Often, people facing
such a decision have tremendous pressure bearing down on
them by the pain and the worry of being a burden to others
that they are not able to make a decision with a clear head. It
is difficult for someone who is that ill to have the fortitude to
fight for his health. It's easier to give up. So I don't think a
request to suicide means he is embracing his own death as
much as it means he is giving up living because it hurts too
much. We don't want to feel pain, especially when it is
relentless.

I remember one day when I went to the doctor. He asked
how I felt, and I told him, "I feel like shit." That was the day I
was diagnosed with cancer. The way I felt, I could've taken a
pill right then to kill myself, and I told him so.

He said, "We're going to take care of that." During the
time I was at home going through the recovery process and
so damn sick, I sometimes thought I'd rather die because I
didn't think I could take it anymore. So it's from a point of
personal experience as well as metaphysical knowledge that I
say the best thing we can do for those who find themselves in
this state is to improve pain management, not help them take
their life prematurely. If your body has not shut down
completely on its own, there is still something left here for
you to do.

A natural death in its proper timing is beautiful, loving,
warm, etheric, and you wonder why you were afraid of it. I
think those who, either through experience or belief

structure, embrace the idea of death as a natural passage and not as a painful end live their lives more deeply.

There are cultures where death is done more consciously. Among the American Indians, the elderly who knew they were dying of natural causes (not the sick, because they always tried to heal their people and did a good job) were not taken along if the tribe moved from one place to another. They were left behind, and someone stayed with them until they died. Then the person who had stayed with them buried the deceased and went on to meet up again with the tribe. China used to have death houses. If you were going to die as a result of old age or illness, your family would take you to a death house, and you'd be put to bed and be made as comfortable as possible, while family waited outside in a garden. The parallel to this is the American hospital.

The best thing we can do to bring about a good death is to live a quality life in as full consciousness as we can bring ourselves to bear. Look at your struggles—depression, fear, anger, or any issue or limitation you feel is blocking your progress toward living a fulfilling life. There, you will find your life challenge. Look at what makes you deeply happy—and I'm not talking about pleasure but the deeper feelings of fulfillment. That is where you need to be going. Meet your challenges with hope, enthusiasm, and the knowledge that you have chosen them, and you will be headed in the right direction. Know that you would not be here doing this if you were not capable of succeeding. Live well, love deeply, and embrace it all.

Then, when you are ready to die, when you can look back at your struggles and see them as being sincerely met, when you feel your life has been well-lived and is complete, then you can think about how you want to die—but not beforehand. To do it beforehand means there is something wrong with the quality of your living.

I think that saying we actually plan our death may be a bit misleading. Since nothing occurs to us that we do not initiate, we are the prime responsible party. But you can plan how your death will be. One way to get comfortable with your actual moment of death is to think about how you would like it to be. Most of us would agree on some general terms: We want it light and easy, gentle, and without pain. But what about the details? Do you want to be alone? Do you want family to be a part of the experience or just nearby? Do you want your hand to be held until you finally depart? Do you want music playing? Do you want the smell of Mom's apple pie wafting from the kitchen to your bedroom?

We are also capable of bringing about our own death without it being a suicidal experience. It is done by giving up spirit through various stages. It's a strange feeling if you manage to let yourself go there and realize you can complete it. The reason most of us don't die that way is that it scares us. My own ideal way to die is to lie down, go to sleep, and make the transition.

A specific case of dying consciously might be found in the life and death of Art Cooper. Art was the managing editor for *GQ Magazine* for twenty years. Two weeks after he wrote his last editor's column saying he was stepping down and turning over the reins, he went to have lunch at the Four Seasons in New York. He had a stroke at the table and died. This is not unusual. How many people have acquired some status in their field, and after having done it for a number of years, "retire" and shortly afterwards die? It's not because they didn't have something to keep them active, but because, quite often, the person has an integral knowledge that they have gone the distance. Again, there are only two reasons you die: Either, you have done what you came to do, or circumstances have changed, usually by your own doing, such that you cannot do what you came to do. I think in the cases of Art Cooper, Winston Churchill, and others of that ilk, they knew that they had finished. Is it planned death? I think it is in the sense that they did what they came to do, and there wasn't anything left at that time for them to further themselves.

I would like to have the sense that I will have left behind my footprint, and anyone who passes by can look at it and do whatever he wishes. Some might step on it to compare it with their own, others might want to rub it out, and some might just want to note that I had come that way. Your footprint is the record of your living, and your death will be the final touch. Do it well.

We die well, die consciously, by living well, living consciously. Prepare for death by living the greatest possible life you can put together. If you love the life you're living, you can't help but love the life you will die to.

NINE

Grief

No one ever told me that grief felt so like fear.

—C.S. Lewis

One of the most painful life events we confront is the death of a loved one, which usually launches us into thorny emotional, mental, physical, and financial challenges. Because death is as much a part of the incarnate experience as birth and because most of us will go through the experience of losing a loved one many times over the course of our lifetime, it makes sense for us to get a perspective on what is going on in the grief process.

When a loved one has died and we really comprehend the reality that they will no longer walk beside us in this world, no longer eat dinner with us, no longer be there when we call them on the phone, no longer sleep with us, dance with us, argue with us, or share the day with us, an acute sorrow wells up from the depths of our being. This profound sadness that washes over us is genuine grief. We should let it wash over us. We should feel the sense of devastation and loss freely and deeply, giving it full measure as it arises within us. The only way past is through. The only way back to happiness is by letting ourselves grieve.

Then the pain fades, and we look up and see that the world has not stopped. We can get back in there and live the life that waits for us beyond this grief.

My view differs from the societal view when it comes to the length of time this process should take. I believe it should take only a few weeks. Although it can well up again from time to time in the months and years to follow, especially around holidays and important anniversaries, those episodes should be short-lived. I think that those who still suffer from the death of a loved one months or years after the death are confusing grief with other feelings: resentment that life is not turning out the way one expected, indignation over how the loved one died, or even outrage at the "injustice" of death itself. Grief in this sense is more about one's own feelings of fear. Rather than missing our loved ones, we are grieving for ourselves and the many worries that come to us with their death: This isn't what I had planned. How am I going to carry on? How can she leave now, just when I need her the most? How can he leave me to face this world alone? How can she leave me to raise these children alone? How could he have left me with all this debt? He just went out to buy a lottery ticket, and they shot him! She was so good, she didn't deserve to die! My child isn't supposed to die before I do! Life's not fair! Why me? Often what we think of as grief is right on the edge of rage.

Death is a private matter controlled only by the individual in accord with his or her contract with the Universe. Before each of us incarnated, we signed off on the blueprint. Within that blueprint was the time (although not the condition) of our death, not in terms of days or years but in terms of cycles of completion on our learning task. The point of death will appear in one of those cycles, and we do, on some level, become aware of it as we approach that point. Although another may take part in our death, as is the case in murder, we had already determined it was our time to die; murder was just the means. A murdered woman used her free will to put herself in a situation where she was isolated and in danger because she knew it was her time to die, and this was the vehicle she chose. It was the will of the soldier killed in battle to enter the service in the first place. He put himself where he needed to be. Understand that the method of departure of the individual was done because he wanted it. He was finished with his sojourn on this planet and knew that in order to progress, he would have to leave.

Except in the case of suicide, no one dies prematurely. People die when it is their time. Although sometimes their timing works well for us, often it is not what we would have agreed to, and we're angry. Yet no matter how needy we are, how insistent we are, how nice we are, how much we try to control death with machines that breathe for us and pump our blood, our loved ones will leave when they have completed their cycle here. We may be able to keep a comatose body functioning on a machine, but the truth is our loved one has left.

Certain cultures and religions promote long-term grief, teaching that our happiness will not be found in this world but only when that day comes when we, too, will die and join with our loved ones. Or, they teach that moving on and living our own lives freely and happily is disrespectful to the memory of the dearly departed. Some consider the passing of the loved one the end of the most satisfying phase of their own life, a life they cannot see themselves rebuilding. However, the truth is that if you continue to grieve over those who have died, not only are you holding yourself back, but you are holding them back. They can feel when they are being called back to the incarnate by loved ones left behind. Asking them to stay around and keep us company is one of the worst things we can do to them. It creates a magnetic pull that holds them to us and keeps them from moving on to their own fulfillment. (This also holds true on the incarnate plane as well. If we cling to someone, we hold him back.) As long as we continue to hold on to those who have died with continual yearnings for them to be with us, with requests that they hang around, or with enshrined pictures on the mantle and rooms left untouched, we hinder their development on the other side.

We can also hinder the progress of others, whether they're on the incarnate or discarnate, with hate. Hate generates more magnetic energy than any other emotional state. When you hate someone and you express it, that enormous magnetic energy reaches him. If I was in that degree of emotion of hating someone, he would feel it in one way or another coming out as a manifestation in his life, whether he's incarnate or discarnate. Putting forth that kind of negativity is interfering and disruptive. It will also catch you up in your own karma, and you better believe you're going to pay. Cause and effect, that's the Law.

For those left behind, the single most important task is to let go. We must allow our loved ones the emotional freedom not only to be who they are but to die when and how they choose. Understand that the when and how of death is the natural outworking of life. Grieve, feel the loss of them, let them go with your blessings and your love, and move on to what life has in store for you next. In freeing them, you free yourself.

Grieving tends to be more difficult for men. Because men are supposed to be strong and resilient and not show emotions considered weak—sadness, fear, etc.—they hold in their feelings or go off by themselves to grieve. They are also less likely to discuss the loss afterwards and refer to it infrequently. That does not mean they have cleared the issue inwardly. In most cases, they haven't and continue to suffer in silence, an unhealthy and debilitating practice. Women tend to be more open about their loss and to grieve openly. I think these differences go back to ancient times and have become a part of our genetic history. Although during my lifetime men tend to cry more openly over loss than they used to, the attitude that crying is a sign of weakness for a man still predominates.

Losing a life partner tends to be a greater problem for men than for women. Men think that they are probably going to die first, and the wife will carry on. (If that weren't true, he wouldn't go through all the preparations of setting up his wife financially upon his death.) When it doesn't happen that way, it's an enormous loss to him because he has a greater internal dependency on his female partner than the female has on him. The female partner is generally the one who gives comfort, support, caring, healing, loving, and sexuality. As a life partner, she's a wonderful provider. Certainly if his partner comes down with an illness, he would take care of her, but in most cases, it is the woman who takes care of the man. When he loses her, his grief, beyond loss of companionship, is usually founded on the loss of emotional support and encouragement, and he may look for relief in alcohol, in drugs, or by burying himself in work—anything to ease the pain. His grief is not just about losing his friend but about losing much that he had depended upon to get through the day. The man who is still pulling out pictures of his deceased wife several years after her death is someone looking for recognition of his pain. He is looking to be soothed. The grief is for his own benefit, to gain something he needs, not really for the person who has died. To move beyond the death of his partner, he must first recognize that what he is really feeling may be fear, anger, betrayal, or victimization. Then, he must work on letting go of his partner and moving on with his own life. The widower is more likely than a widow to find himself a new mate.

When a man dies, beyond genuine grief, the woman's issues tend to be more external. How she is affected by his death and how she responds depend a lot on her financial condition when he dies. If the elements necessary for her continued lifestyle are intact, her grief will be more about losing his friendship and companionship and will not be encumbered with anger at being left. However, if she finds herself forced to go out into the workplace when she hasn't worked in years or to find a small apartment in a bad area of town because he left her in financial decline, then her reaction will be more one of anger than genuine grief. I've heard women say, "How dare he die on me!" and "I hope he's in hell for dying!" They're angry at being left in difficult conditions. Women who experience genuine grief at the loss of their partner without the issues of added external burdens often find themselves content to live alone and don't feel the need to run out and look for a new partner. They don't depend on a partner for the emotional support the way a man does. Certainly if someone who pleased her came along, she would act upon that, but usually she doesn't want anyone trying to set her up with someone else. Many women are in the workplace and are content with their cat, their dog, their bird, and their garden.

It will be different for her, however, if she stays in the house in which they had spent many years together. She can expect stronger emotional reactions and an upwelling of grief as she continues to sleep in the bedroom he shared with her, eat in the kitchen where they cooked and ate meals together, and walk through the living room where they shared holidays and evenings. Family and friends calling upon her can help considerably. Also helpful is being near family and friends and in a place where she is well-established. A woman in this situation has everything she needs, she just doesn't have him.

Losing a mother seems to be more difficult than losing a father. Tears are shed over both parents, but the children tend to think of the father, remember him softly, recall the funny or smart things he did or said, and his death is more acceptable to them. They miss him, and that's it. Not so with mom. Pain over losing mom lasts a long time. From birth, to being taught how to eat and walk, to getting pulled out of trouble, mom was usually the one there first, so the emotional ties were more complex and the relationship was usually closer and more engaged. In addition to genuine grief, when parents die, often the first thing that comes to mind is, "What am I going to do?" They are no longer around to give that extra hug, extra knowledge, or extra financial support. The only way the grief over their death can be set in its rightful place is when the offspring know, or eventually figure out, that they are able to develop their own self-sufficiency and carry on. Otherwise, the losses will hold them back.

For those who have lost someone in especially shocking or difficult circumstances—murder or accident—I hope they can find consolation in the fact that their loved one's spirit knew the blueprint. We each make choices that will advance us, including choosing what lesson we are here to learn and when we will have reached that point. Once we have reached it, we can only continue our development by going to the discarnate side of the school. I think there would be less fear of death if people understood that particular metaphysical reality. We are where we're supposed to be at the time we're supposed to be there. If that means I get shot in a hold-up at the convenience store when I go in to buy a lottery ticket, then so be it. As harsh as it may sound, I accepted that time of death and way of dying. I then move on to the next phase of my development. No one can take anyone's life without the consent of our consciousness. Our bottom line is our commitment to the fulfillment of the lifeline. If we fight off the attacker, then we were supposed to win. If we don't and we die from the attack, then that was when we agreed the lifeline would end and we would depart.

Losing a loved one to suicide is especially difficult. In addition to the grief we feel, a loved one's suicide can leave us riddled with guilt, anger, shame, and confusion. There are many resources out there offering help. What I would add is that you can still give your loved one help from here by sending him thoughts and spoken words aimed at elevating him and putting him in the light. Do not criticize him for the suicide, but rather, try to raise his consciousness so that he can get into a frame of mind where the etheric workers can make contact and help him move from where he is trapped below the line. Tell him that he is not where he is supposed to be. Tell him to look around, that there is someone there to help him. Your thoughts to him should be uplifting and loving, pointing him to go on his way. In doing this, you not only help him, but you help yourself as well. Then let him go with love and blessings.

Grieving in a healthy way means learning how to give our love freely, without expectations, control, or emotional dependency. In so doing, when a loved one dies, we can heal the genuine grief more quickly and move on to continue a fulfilling and satisfying life. Avail yourself of therapeutic help if you feel it would be useful. I would also like to add that in moments of despair, you have inner resources. There is, inside of you, a part that is wise enough and strong enough to overcome anything. This is your soul, your spirit, your consciousness. Recognizing this does not require a change of religion but perhaps a change of orientation. Talk to your inner self and connect to the Universe in thought and prayer. In this way you connect to the higher power, of which you are a part. Do not doubt it. The Universe is pure, truthful, and loving, and you are an integral part of it.

Only when grief is fully realized can you appreciate its gift—love fully experienced. There is happiness after death, both for those who die and for those left behind. Love and freedom show the way. Believe.

TEN

Nature and Humankind
A Relationship Made in Heaven

God is the great mysterious motivator of what we call
nature, and it has been said often by philosophers, that
nature is the will of God. And, I prefer to say that nature is
the only body of God that we shall ever see.

—Frank Lloyd Wright

Whenever we desire, we can wrap ourselves in the sensual experience of this planet's abundant and diverse composition. We can walk among ancient trees, deep grasses, and colorful flowers; lose ourselves to the sound of the mesmerizing surf or a sweet birdsong; fall under the spell of a soft rain, a fragrant wind, or the deep silence of a snowfall; or commune with our favorite animal. Nature is intimately partnered with us in this physical experience, and that is perhaps the greatest boon of our incarnate existence, as nature is directly connected to and informed by the Universe.

Some of our most endearing partners are our pets. After a difficult day, they are there waiting for us, ready to fulfill our desire to feel all-giving and unconditionally accepting energy. Isn't that what love is all about? They accept our tears, soothe our angst, and make us laugh. They ask for nothing and give everything.

What separates humans from animal, mineral, and plant life is that animals, minerals, and vegetation do not have consciousness, as such. They must follow basic patterns inherent in their make-up; whereas, a human can make judgments and exercise free will to act in various ways for many different reasons. Because we have consciousness and they do not, we are responsible for their care.

Every animal responds to its human keeper, one way or another, just as a garden or home responds to the care it is given. And although we can give animals a lot of love, they are animals and they must follow their own part in the cycle of nature. They do not have consciousness beyond what is required for them to follow their instincts. You might ask why, then, can your pet look at you with such "soulful" eyes. What you are seeing is a reflection of yourself, a reflection of your love, affection, and goodness—or of your anger, frustration, and irritation. You can only see what you are, what you have developed yourself to be. This is true whether we're talking about what we see in our animals or what we see in our family, friends, neighbors, and work associates. That is all we are capable of seeing, experiencing, and interacting with in any given moment.

When a human dies, he makes the transition to the other side with his consciousness intact. He then engages in the discarnate side of the school, and at some later point, reincarnates. On the other hand, animals and the other elements of the nature pool of this planet have a different system. Each aspect of nature goes through the cycle fundamental to its element. Trees, bushes, and flowers are seasonal, and animals are born, age, and die. When they die, all elements of nature are returned to the nature pool, where their energy can be used for whatever needs to be generated. The energy of a butterfly can be used in the creation of an elephant. The energy of a cactus can be used toward the manifestation of a fish. The energy of our pet can be put back into the pool and used to create a flower, a storm, an ant, or a tree.

When a pet dies, we usually experience a deep grief, especially if the animal has been part of our life for a number of years. But again, it is my belief that normal grief does not exceed a few weeks. After that, what is being experienced is something other than grief. Grief that lasts for months or years after the pet's death implies an unhealthy dependency on that animal. Our interaction with our pets should never substitute for interacting with our fellow humans. Yet some people get so attached to their animals and make them such a significant part of their psychological support structure that when the animal is no longer there, the person goes to pieces. If you find yourself grieving for an animal, go through the mourning, but limit its time and release your attachment to the animal.

In the negative realms of the discarnate world, there are no animals as pets because there is no energy there to maintain them. However, if a person in the negative discarnate has a clear fear of animals or a deep aversion to a particular animal, he would project that fear in the discarnate and the animal would appear as being real and as monstrous as the fear that conjures it. It is not real but simply a projection of what the individual has in his mind and has created as part of his distorted expectation of the afterlife.

In the positive planes of the discarnate, because we are developing our relationships with other conscious beings, we usually do not feel a desire to develop a relationship with the energy pool that is nature except as an expression of creativity. Although we could project an image of an animal to our liking and it would appear real to us, it would really be nothing more than our own projection. In the Earth School, animals function as companions and stabilizers, and in the positive discarnate, we do not have a need for animal companionship or a need to ground our energy. In time, as we adapt to being back in the discarnate form, we come to understand this in the same way that we eventually understand how we do not have to eat corn-on-the-cob anymore to survive. Animals are designed for the incarnate planes of the Earth School, and that is where they best serve and provide the most fulfillment.

Nature, Our Divine Tool

The fundamental structure of the Universe is one of harmony. Every being, creature, rock, and blade of grass — as well as every galaxy, planet, and asteroid — *everything* in this harmonious Universe is observed and given sponsorship and guidance. When the Earth School was formed, it too was in harmony under perfect Universal conditions. Vegetation was profuse and healthy, and beasts lived side by side and did not eat one another.

Nature was then made subject to humankind's dominion. When we were made physically manifest here, we agreed to take responsibility for the administration of the planet and were given the ability to have a direct impact on nature. Because it is inherent within nature to stay in balance with the harmonious frequency of the Universe, when we do something that sets things off balance, nature must respond by trying to put things back in balance. Our disharmonious administration of the planet causes us all — humans and the rest of the earth — to lose that balance. And nature ever operates to put things right.

Although it can act to rebalance an inequality we have created, nature does not have direct input into us and cannot directly act upon us as beings. For example, if we pull up grass, the response of the area where we pulled the grass would be to rebalance itself, not act upon us. We can put pesticide on a field, and the field's response is to rebalance itself, not to degerm us. In our interactions with nature, humankind has the authority, meaning the direct input. We walk on the grass; pick and eat fruits and vegetables; breed, raise, and eat animals; engage in genetic engineering; and drill for oil and minerals. Nature cannot step up and act upon us, except as it must respond to its basic need to be in balance. We have the power either to create a flourishing cornucopia of life to nurture and support us or to create hurricanes, melting polar ice caps, and swarms of locusts.

The energy to generate plant and animal life on this planet comes from the nature pool—an infinite source of energy connected to this school, the natural life force of this planet. All planets have their nature pools. Even those that appear to have no growth have basic natural elements, although considerably different from ours. These nature pools operate in accord with harmonious Universal Law, and it is impossible for us to interfere with the perfect functioning of this co-creative process of the Infinite Mind.

Like everything in the Universe, nature pools are energies that respond, give, and ask nothing in return. Energy from Earth's nature pool is used, transformed, and molded into whatever forms are required to respond to the acts of man and nature on this planet. From moths to moose, from sand and oceans to mountains and roses, with the exception of the human body, all life forms on this planet are generated from the nature pool. This energy is ever available and responsive to planetary events. If we nurture and energize a hundred acres through good care and good farming methods, then the nature pool will be there to supply the natural energy to bring the vegetation into full flower. If we kill off a hundred acres of vegetation in such a way that it won't grow again, the energy reflects that change and does not supply what is needed for that area to reestablish growth. As man becomes more refined, nature reacts accordingly. When man was living in caves and using sticks and stones as tools, we had dinosaurs. As man changed, the dinosaurs disappeared. Now we have poodles.

The design of the planet is such that each aspect of nature serves a function. The function of minerals is to focus the natural force. Minerals are like the earth's blood and carry great power. When jewels are used as protection, they tend to focus the natural force of the wearer and provide a shield against any intrusion. That is why jewels have always been thought of as having great power — they do. That power is constant, even if the owner decides to use it for ill gain. (But remember, karma prevails, and what is sent out will return.)

Plants serve as food and medicine for us and for the animals. Food stabilizes. Do you recall ever having an upset stomach and some of the old-fashioned remedies helped make you feel better? Many plants and foods have medicinal properties, and some even have hallucinogenic properties. Vegetation has a wide range of uses from medicinal to coloring to keeping us warm in the winter and dry in the rainy season. The plant world is an amazing toolbox for the human being. Everything we need to survive can be found growing from the earth.

Animals are here as companions and stabilizers. Having a direct connection to the earth, they serve the important function of being able to ground and stabilize our energies by taking our excess energy and feeding it back into the earth. They — along with plants — absorb a lot of negative energy. As we nurture and care for them, they leave us calmer in the midst of our sometimes chaotic incarnate experience. That is why they are so comforting to be around when we are stressed or despondent. It is a pleasant process for the animal as well. Even wild animals have this function, but we have thrown off their ability to trust us by our own violence and killing. Because nature must respond to our input, when we started eating flesh, not only did animals stop trusting us, but we set into motion the manifestation of carnivorous animals. The more negative human consciousness becomes, the more negative and aggressive animals become. We control that by how we think and treat the creatures. We can wipe out a whole species, or we can populate the earth with nothing but cats. It is up to us.

Earth was formed in harmony, and then man was formed in harmony and given the ability and responsibility for administering himself and the planet. He was left to do what he would. Originally on this planet, humankind held a greater respect for and appreciation of nature in this tremendous ongoing creative act. People did not eat animals, animals did not eat other animals, and vegetation grew in great profusion. In the original, harmonious format of life on this planet, the way we now feel about our pets is what we felt for all of nature—great appreciation, respect, and affection. Carnivores, killer storms, droughts, plagues, disease ... none of these were in the original design. They are the results of man's disharmonious actions and nature's need to rebalance itself. The imbalances we've created have caused polluted air and water, plants that won't grow, and food that doesn't satisfy.

If we were the strong planet we could be, galactic events would not have the impact on us that they do. On many parts of the planet, we have created a situation where the collective consciousness is more negative than positive. A collective state of consciousness that is negative attracts negative energy to itself. Because of this, we attract from the reaches of space ripples of energy that cause our natural disasters. When we compound the negative collective consciousness with the ignorant act of building flimsy housing for people to live in, we have multitudes dying from just one earthquake.[6]

---

[6] Another component of those deaths is that each of those thousands of people had arrived at a point in their individual life learning lesson where they had either reached the apex of their learning on that lesson or they could no longer progress. What the earthquake did was provide the means for the death but not the reason. If they still have learning to do, they will not be a casualty of the earthquake. Most of us would not consciously choose to die from a catastrophe. We would choose to die peacefully and quietly in our own bed. The fact that so many of us die violently and suddenly is

Although these ripples of energy would still have an impact on the planet even if our collective consciousness were more positive, the impact would not be as disastrous because the positive energy would absorb the waves of energy with minimal reaction by the earth and render their effects less catastrophic. The more positive the collective consciousness, the more harmonious the planet. Life responds to us and reflects us directly. If we are beautiful, our surroundings are beautiful. If we are ugly and mean, our surroundings, including the animals in our life, will reflect that.

Restoring Harmony

If we wish to make our planet the Eden it can be, there are things we can do, and nature will respond to our input. Closely examine your own environment and the impact you are having on the natural world. Also, consider harmonious ways you can address the larger, careless acts that are destructive of nature—such as destroying acres of trees to build inferior housing or carelessly polluting the water in the process of building a new gadget. Finally, you can deepen your personal relationship with the natural world.

First, examine your own environment. Would you call your home harmonious? Do you feel a sense of peace and comfort when you're there? Fill your home with nature's beauty. Pets, plants, and other natural elements provide visual harmony. Consider how different it feels to enter into a bare room with only a couple of pieces of saggy furniture than to enter into a room that has arrangements of furniture, flourishing plants, a bowl of colorful stones, a tank full of vibrant fish, a cat napping by the fireplace, and a dog sleeping curled up where the sunlight hits the floor. Such a room visually, and viscerally, draws you in and reminds you

another indicator of the state of our being unconscious to our personal potential and life's purpose.

of your spiritual and physical connection to nature and the Universe. Create harmony in your home.

If you have a yard, is it well-tended? Take care of your property, and bring it to its higher level of manifestation. Plant flowers and plants, place rocks, and put up a birdbath. Be careful of the means you use to maintain your yard. Soaking the ground with weed killer is harmful to nature, because that ground will be foul for years. But in pulling a weed, you do not hurt nature. If you cut back a hedge growing wild, you're not hurting the hedge. In fact, you may actually be promoting its higher development, because cutting it back helps the hedge respond to a more intense growth pattern.

Our housing can be energy-efficient, and we can be using natural energy sources, such as solar and wind. We can build houses using natural elements derived from and in harmony with the local environment. On the other hand, if you clear ten acres of trees and vegetation to build inferior housing for profit, then you're hurting nature and your fellow human beings just for money. There will be unpleasant karmic consequences.

Another issue is our raising of animals for food. Is that immoral in terms of being the masters of this planet? I would think it is. Personally, I would rather live in a world where animals were not raised and used for food. However, most of us on this planet come from genetic lines that have been eating the flesh of animals for thousands of years, and our bodies have adapted so that they function best when they take in some animal flesh. It is true that there are tribes and even entire countries of people who have eaten only vegetation for generations, and they tend to be healthier and live longer. But it takes a minimum of seven generations for most of us meat-eaters to make the transition from non-animal to fundamentally vegetarian before we can produce a child who can be a vegetarian and still function optimally.

My personal observation is that those who try to make the transition from eating meat to vegetarianism within their own lifetime, although they appear to be reasonably healthy, seem to become slower in their thought process and much slower in their body coordination. (On the other hand, it has also been my observation that those who are heavy meat-eaters tend to be dense in their thinking process). However, we can change our diet so that the proportion of meat we eat is less, and each generation can improve on the mix of meat to vegetation so that eventually we can all be vegetarians without giving up optimal functioning.

Our role with nature is to work in harmony with it to bring its elements to the highest degree of their manifestation. We can learn to do that the way a botanist would by raising a group of plants under ideal conditions to have them produce the greatest flowers, leaves, or fruits. We can also study how nature puts it together without our interference by observing areas of profuse natural growth. The negative forces of nature—such as fire ants, venomous snakes, and so on—are a result of man's negative consciousness. If we wish to eradicate such negative forces, there are two things we can do. First, we can adjust our thoughts, feelings, and actions, and thus our consciousness, to be more positive. Second, we can use natural forces against them. Science realized, for example, that if we want to get rid of the tsetse fly, which spreads malaria, we have to take away its ability to reproduce. This is more effective than killing them off directly because nature pool energy does not lend itself to a species that is not reproducing.

So many of us believe that we're impotent when it comes to solving the larger problems of the world. Yet there is nothing impotent about the human mind. Even if you're not the type of person to write letters or join protests, if you feel deeply about an issue, you can dedicate a period of time every day—five or ten minutes, sixty seconds even—when you sit still and send out your objection in a thought process. Then hold in your mind a feeling of appreciation of, respect for, and harmony with the Earth. If ninety-two million people did that, change for the better would be inevitable and swift.

This planet is here to provide a classroom for learning experiences for individual consciousness, and we are co-creators with Omnipotent Intelligence. In the co-creative process, we exercise our free will, which cannot be interfered with by *any* power, higher or lower. If we decide to create in a negative form, nothing will stop us. Every day, we consciously create negativity. How many people are angry in any given moment? Millions per second maybe? That anger, the thought and the feeling of it, is negative energy emitted into the ethers, and energy doesn't die. We need to fully comprehend that the Universe has no limits. It is ever-expansive. Every thought we have and every word we speak goes out into this infinite Universe and stays there.

Every thought we have has an effect on us and our planet as well. We can be mindful of our thoughts. Every time we indulge in negative thought, we produce disharmony on both the non-physical (or non-visible) level as well as the manifested level. Our effect is enormous. Commuting negative thoughts to positive ones would begin to change the world from what it is to the place it was originally intended to be—a place of graciousness, compassion, harmony, and beauty.

Any time that we need to reconnect with the harmony, we can go outside to appreciate and interact with nature: taking a walk in a beautiful park, swimming in a lake, climbing a mountain, trekking in the desert, or caring for animals. All of these activities help us connect to nature and, in turn, to the harmonious Universal energy that informs it.

Consider the sweet, loving rapport we have with our pets. Steep yourself in that feeling for a moment. This is the feeling we should have for every tree, flower, and bird that passes into our life. This is the feeling that should navigate our dominion over Earth's natural kingdom. This is the feeling that will develop in us a deeper awareness of the more subtle, energetic aspects of nature, our intimate partner in this physical experience. Nature's promise awaits you. Take a walk, look around, listen, smell, taste. Appreciate. *Feel* it.

ELEVEN

Graduation

*The human mind is not capable of grasping the Universe.
We are like a little child entering a huge library. The walls
are covered to the ceilings with books in many different
tongues. The child knows that someone must have written
these books. It does not know who or how. It does not
understand the languages in which they are written. But the
child notes a definite plan in the arrangement of books – a
mysterious order which it does not comprehend, but only
dimly suspects.*

— Albert Einstein

Ever-unfolding discovery. Nothing in the Universe lies
outside this purpose. We can think of the Universe as one
great school offering limitless opportunities to explore,
discover, and learn. The learning opportunities are offered
through a series of smaller schools, or galaxies, with each
devoted to a different focus and pattern of study. As each of
us expands our knowledge, we feed our experience of
wisdom, spiced with our unique quality of being, into the
Universal whole.

What we learn and how we contribute is always up to us.
That is the Universe's ultimate gift—free will. What informs
our decisions is the pain of our ignorance. Which schools we
attend and why we have chosen to participate in the Earth
School at this time are not determined by the knowledge we
already have but by what we don't yet know. Imagine a
seesaw, with our ignorance represented by the part

suspended in air. When we bring knowledge to bear on it, that end of the seesaw tilts down. However, as we gain knowledge, the other end of the seesaw tilts up into the air — yet more ignorance. The pain you experience is your ignorance holding itself up to you so that you may find the knowledge it requires. There is always an opportunity to learn when you're ready. Our particular ignorance leads us to our next school, next lifetime, next family, next mate, next job, next health challenge, next drama, or next crossroad.

Each of us has come to this point in the Universe to school ourselves in the art of adaptation. Adaptation is required of everyone here, be they sitting upon a royal throne or falling down drunk in the gutter. We all arrived here with such diverse learning backgrounds and for a variety of reasons. Our common link is that the exquisite quality of the Earth School can meet our individual needs.

Earth is an advanced school with interesting learning criteria. First, it's physical. That's pretty exciting, because operating a physical vehicle is about as tricky as operating an interstellar spaceship. We also deal with two different types of physical vehicles, male and female, and it sometimes takes well into adulthood to learn how to manage that. Not only do we deal with the physical world, but we also have mental activity to experience and manage. Because this school deals with a broad range of information, our mental activity brings us countless variations, a lot of them invisible. This is an amazingly intricate place of learning.

An old law of metaphysics declares that what is true of the whole is true of the part, and what is true of the part is true of the whole. Always. We are a microcosmic reflection of the Universe itself, individualized expressions of the whole, from which we can never be separated. We have always been and will always be.

Your own consciousness is your direct relationship to the Universe. What your consciousness cares about is the pursuit of wisdom. Your body, on the other hand, belongs to the planet. What the body cares about are the issues of survival: Am I safe? Do I have enough to eat? Is there a roof over my head? Do I have money in my pocket? Consciousness looks at the body and says, "Survival? What are you talking about? I have always been and I will always be. What is this survival thing?" Consciousness is not concerned about the mundane realities. It is part and parcel of Universal Mind and knows that all things are supplied and that there is never a shortage. The body looks at consciousness and says, "Hey, if I can't eat it, wear it, or drive it, I don't have any use for it." Our consciousness and our body have different agendas.

Yet in this particular school, the only way consciousness can develop wisdom is through physical experience, and the body is the necessary format. We are here to learn issues of materiality and mass and how to function within definitive limitations. Our body cannot go without food indefinitely or walk through walls. It must be taken into account when developing the mind and spirit. This school offers a range of opportunities for working through limitations and creating within that framework.

In addition to our body, the tools of our consciousness include our soul and our personality. Soul is a part of your consciousness. It sees the human element every day and motivates you to move in the direction and take the actions that will result in your highest good. Soul can be looked at as the intermediary between consciousness and our human aspect. Your personality can be thought of as the mind aspect of your body, the result of what you manifest in body, mind, and soul. It is your own reflection of the mundane world you live in and is shaped in large part by the choices you make.

It is the planet's responsibility, and that of society as a whole, to help point out our specific ignorance and show us what it is we're here to do. Unfortunately, the way society runs the school is by reverse process—instead of showing you how things work, it shows what doesn't work and what to stay away from. For many of us, the lessons begin like the first day of school. The school bully hits you in the nose. That tells you that you had better stay away from the school bully. Then that handsome dark-haired boy with the great smile or the pretty girl with the braids becomes an ache in your heart. You have to figure out what to do with that feeling. If the teacher is gruff and insensitive, you have to learn how to deal with that. Although this adverse method of learning does not really help us move on to our specific learning experience, it does show us a lot about what doesn't work.

After we make our passage through the first year of school (i.e., the first lifetime), and we return to the etheric side, chances are that we feel great relief at getting out of here. We may decide it was a rotten trip and that going to that part of the school wasn't a good idea. Things on the etheric side are as great as they were before we left for the incarnate side of the school, and before long, we're feeling fulfilled in our learning and pastimes there. We don't have to worry about things like rent and groceries. There is no division of male and female and no negativity to work around. Everything flows in sweet harmony, and soon we forget how tough it was on the incarnate side. In no time at all, we don't think about it anymore.

But the day rolls around when we become aware of a deep ache. The seesaw is still out of kilter, and something has to be done about it. We go to the wise school administrators and tell them of our terrible pain. The wise doctors say, "We've got just the thing for you. It's called reincarnation."

Well our ignorance is in sore need of relief, and by this time, we've experienced such a rejuvenation that we think it sounds like just what we're looking for. "How do we do it?" we ask. The Reincarnation Board draws up another program of study for us on the incarnate side, they design another body vehicle for us, and they give us the blueprint of the life that can guide us to the knowledge we seek. We review it, recognize the wisdom of their plan, and agree to it. So begins another incarnation.

You might wonder if the school was originally designed to be such a struggle. It shouldn't be, but it is because we have perpetuated the struggle. In this difficult school, it is easy to get lost in that mundane world of the body and personality and forget the larger consciousness that we are. We quickly lose ourselves in the rudiments of physical existence. We come to believe in, and thus feel, lack. We cheat. We try to control others. We give in to despair. We even murder. We stagnate in survival mode and stop learning, which causes us to shrivel up and become as lifeless as we can ever really become. We put a barrier between ourselves and Universal reality because we are not pursuing knowledge. That is not to say, however, that the intellectual who pursues a singular line of learning brings himself any closer to developing awareness of Universal reality. In his obsession, he too becomes lost in a narrow existence.

To realize Universal reality, we need only open ourselves to our innate, insatiable curiosity to seek the broader knowledge of many things—then to embrace the adventure. Then we will know ourselves as children of the Universe. The athlete who finally masters a physical feat, the shy person who goes to the party and has a good time, or the mathematician who solves a complex theoretical problem all experience that gratifying sense of accomplishment wrought through effort and learning. Each brings to this sense of accomplishment his or her unique self-realization. When we have such moments, we feel larger, smarter, more empowered—all feelings that bring us into harmony with and deepen our connection to the Universal Source. At this moment, billions of souls—each a microcosm of the greater, harmonious Universe—are transporting themselves over this planet on their individual journeys to wisdom and enlightenment. Every bit of knowledge we gather is a bit of knowledge that, once ingested into our life as reality, brings us to a closer understanding of the infinite power, wisdom, and love we call God.

God is the very source energy of the Universe, the I Am, the essence of what we consider ultimate good. There cannot be a complete definition of God, only a knowing that it exists. God has to be understood by feeling, by impress, rather than by definition, and every person is going to experience and understand it differently. As well as opening ourselves to learning and adventure, to feel God's impress, we must learn true self-acceptance. Acceptance means to receive gladly. The more you receive yourself gladly and the more you accept yourself for who and what you are, the more love comes to you, and the more it issues forth from you. You begin to become aware of yourself in your full totality, your full meaning in this Universe, and a glimpse of the bigger picture becomes available to you. The person who accepts himself is a deeply loving person because he has no fear, no need to compete, and no grasping need for recognition; he is self-contained. A self-accepting person is dynamic. He is someone who easily and freely expresses who he is and generously gives of his life. Of course, he will have idiosyncrasies that others may look at and say they wouldn't want to tolerate. That's okay with him because he knows that if he finds his idiosyncrasies too daunting to live with, he can change them. Self-acceptance, or self-love, is the reflection of the very character of the Universe. It is the motivation behind life in its highest manifestation. Self-love is the willingness to accept yourself *as you are*, with the understanding that *as you are* is an ongoing work in awareness. Everything you do unfolds a chapter or opens a door that says, "Here's a new view of what you are." That is the ongoing and wondrous discovery of our Self.

Built within each of us is the knowledge of who we are and what we wish to create in this life, as well as a willingness to embrace whatever that experience brings us. How can we know if we are on the right path? We can know it when our life reflects the quality of joyous discovery. It isn't so much about having a happy day as it is an inner quality of life that makes you glad you're participating with yourself and with the world in the opportunities presenting themselves to you. The person who sees and embraces opportunity feels the excitement of a child scrambling over the hilltop to see what else there is to participate in. Mystery and discovery keep us going. And no one else can discover what we can, for each of us brings awareness and knowledge peculiar to our own desires and patterns of growth. The Universe backs our personal experience of discovery by providing all of the elements necessary for our success. The more we embrace life, the more the Universe can support us.

What is the reward? In the moment you relieve your ignorance, when you no longer feel any pain, you commune directly with the Source of the Universe. That is Nirvana of all nirvanas, the transcendental awareness of all transcendental awareness. It is life in its purest form.

We cannot, however, stay in this state indefinitely, only long enough to fulfill our appetite for that blissful communion. Then off we go, and soon we're hungry again. When that time comes, we are inspired to take the steps to answer our newly revealed ignorance. It is unbounded discovery.

In the long run, then, it behooves us to have a good time on our sojourn here. The Universe directly responds to our input, so as more of us bring in positive thinking, positive action, and positive interaction, the better things become. Here are some suggestions for having a more joy-filled, fulfilling experience at the Earth School.

First, love it. It only makes sense to love where you are. Appreciation and gratitude bring us back to our natural, harmonious state of joy. Hating where you are only feeds the pain of your ignorance. Remember, no one sent you here. You chose to come here. For whatever time you're here, this is your home. Cherish it.

Second, remember that you are a unique individual with your own curriculum. No one has ever used that curriculum before, and no one ever will again. That makes your studies here strictly independent, uniquely you, and equal in importance to everyone else's studies. Although you might like reviewing your lessons with those around you, never expect them to understand them as you do or to do your work for you.

Third, have fun. Like any good school, built into the system are lunch breaks, rest times, games, field trips, silly pranks, dances, concerts, class plays, and more. If you always study without bothering to look up and relish the sheer fun and joy being offered to you, your experience here will be tedious, stale, and draining. Learning is supposed to be fun. When you know it's time to go out and play, by all means do so. Restore yourself. Then, as with any other responsibility awaiting you, recognize when playtime is over and hit the books again.

Fourth, don't spend your energy and your life trying to figure out when you're going to leave this school for good. No one can tell you that. You will leave here only when the pain of your ignorance is healed, your hunger is satiated, and you have become intelligent enough to be graduated. Each of us has unique learning requirements, and it can take anywhere from a few decades to a couple of billion years to complete our coursework here. Too many of us gripe and groan about getting out of here. Such thinking only wastes valuable opportunities. Catch yourself whenever you fall into this kind of negative thought pattern. What aren't you seeing? What aren't you allowing into your experience? Especially when you are in great pain, ask for help to see the answer you seek. Our experience here is supposed to be gratifying and joy-filled.

Finally, look at all the dear friends we make along the way.

The Earth School gives us a chance to do things that we can't do anyplace else in the Universe. So what's your hurry? You're going to leave soon enough. For most of us, graduation from high school or college is a time of satisfaction touched with poignancy. We're glad to finish, but it hurts to leave because we're leaving behind some of the best years of our life, some of the best friends we ever made, and great fun. It's no different on the larger scale of the Earth School. Everything we complained and moaned about for thousands of years will come back to us in our wisdom. We will know that it wasn't so bad after all, and we would kind of like to stay here.

How will we know when we're approaching the point of gradation from the Earth School? I believe we will know that time is close when we are able to walk on water, literally. To me, that suggests mastery in this physical world. We will know we are approaching the point of graduation when we operate in full awareness of ourselves as a reflection of the Universe. To me, that demonstrates wisdom of spirit. And we will know we are approaching the point of graduation when we express love freely, openly, and deeply. To me, that represents the very essence of the harmonious heart of Creation.

So whenever you experience fear of dying, I urge you to remember that the Universe continues to support us in the life in the world hereafter. There is joy in dying, and I really mean joy! Don't be afraid — be excited! Dying opens the door to the next thing we have to learn about living. There is as much activity, creativity, involvement, and engagement with learning, living, and loving after death as there is in life. Because your death will be an extension of how you live, if you live well, you will die well.

So step into your life. The answers you seek lie there. The life you are leading, the body you ensoul, and every moment in this wondrous place we call home all work together to create the ideal opportunities for you to manifest your highest and most unique self. As you fully engage life, you will deepen your awareness of that infinite Source of all and bring yourself into intelligent, conscious, blissful communion with it. In each moment, live to the highest quality of your being and experience ultimate self-love. Then, when you have reached the apex of your learning in this life, die in joy and bring these experiences and the wisdom you have gleaned to the table of life in the hereafter and celebrate.

May every moment fill you with wonder.

About the Author

Gregge Tiffen's intensive training in mysticism and mystical law began over fifty years ago in the Far East. He returned to the United States to launch G-Systems International, which has become a respected and accurate source for metaphysical information worldwide. He is a well-known consultant, lecturer, and teacher and has published his work in print and audio formats. Gregge lives in Dallas, Texas and may be reached through his website at www.g-systems.com.

Made in the USA
San Bernardino, CA
14 September 2017